Taking Ethics to Heart

First Published 2004
The Institute of Chartered Accountants of Scotland

ISBN 1 904574 10 6

This book is published for the Research Committee of
The Institute of Chartered Accountants of Scotland
and does not necessarily represent the views of
the Council of the Institute.

No responsibility for loss occasioned to any person acting
or refraining from action as a result of any material
in this publication can be accepted by the author or publisher.

Printed and Bound in Great Britain
by T J International

CONTENTS

FOREWORD

George Bernard Shaw was not an accountant, or a lawyer, doctor or member of any other chartered body for that matter, and so accountants might choose to ignore his aphorism that "all professions are a conspiracy against the laity". But it would be particularly arrogant and unwise to ignore the implicit challenge of his words in this 150th year of the oldest professional accounting body in the world, The Institute of Chartered Accountants of Scotland (ICAS).

The Research Committee of ICAS has undertaken an investigation into the ethical standing of accountants because one of the hallmarks of professionalism is that of maintaining high levels of ethical conduct in whatever working environment accountants find themselves. Even if the ethical standing of the profession were not in question, an examination of ethical issues affecting the profession would always be an appropriate exercise for a professional body. However, the second reason for initiating this investigation is more closely tied to the particular circumstances of the current time. Recent and high profile controversies, such as, but not limited to, Enron and WorldCom, appear to have diminished the ethical standing of accountants in the eyes of the general public. So it is timely to look afresh at the pressures that accountants face in ensuring that ethical standards are maintained and to explore the ways in which individuals, firms, business and the profession itself, with or without wider institutional involvement, can respond creatively and usefully to the pressures its members are under by taking ethics to heart.

The report is set out in two parts. The first part of the report describes the research approach adopted and introduces the issues identified by the research. A key finding is that despite formal ethical guidance by accounting institutes, individually and collectively, there is currently no clear framework used by accountants for ethical decision making. The absence of such a framework makes it extremely difficult for individuals and firms to identify any process that would improve ethical outcomes. This report proposes such a framework and suggests that this would facilitate education and training and greatly assist a consistent and rigorous decision-making process within firms and businesses.

Adopting this framework, the second part looks at possible remedies and actions. Whilst the individual is the focal point for decision making, it is recognised that individuals do not operate in isolation from the business environment in which they work. As a result, any corrective action requires a coordinated approach by individuals, professional bodies and institutions. The suggested remedies are looked at from these different perspectives.

The concluding chapter resummarises the recommendations contained in the second part of the report in a way that allows those accepting responsibility for implementation to coordinate their activities with other stakeholders. This chapter also highlights, and amplifies, the implications of the research finding that there is an identifiable time of maximum ethical complexity in an individual's career to which particular attention is justified.

The Research Committee of The Institute of Chartered Accountants of Scotland is pleased to have had the opportunity to stimulate thinking in this important area at a time when the ethical standing of the profession has been questioned. It recognises that its views do not necessarily represent those of ICAS itself, but considers that the whole accountancy profession is concerned directly, or indirectly, with ethical decision making and hopes that its analysis and recommendations will be the subject of wide consideration by all concerned.

Nigel Macdonald
Convener
Research Committee

October 2004

The Research Committee and the Editors

This discussion document was prepared by the Research Committee of The Institute of Chartered Accountants of Scotland. For the purposes of this project, the Committee consisted of:

Nigel Macdonald	Convener, Research Committee and a Past President of ICAS. Retired, previously Partner, Ernst & Young,
Mark Allison	Executive Director, CA Education, ICAS.
Jan Bebbington	Professor of Accounting and Sustainable Development, University of St Andrews.
Aileen Beattie	Executive Director, Technical Policy, ICAS.
Christine Helliar	Director of Research, ICAS and Professor of Treasury Management, University of Dundee.
Guy Jubb	Investment Director, Standard Life Investments.
Jan Mouritsen	Professor of Management Control, Copenhagen Business School.
David McCraw	Head of Structured Products, Aberdeen Asset Managers Ltd.
Ronald Paterson	Retired, previously Partner, Ernst & Young.
Kenneth Peasnell	Professor of Accounting, University of Lancaster.
Stuart Turley	Professor of Accounting, University of Manchester.

Professor Christine Helliar and Professor Jan Bebbington acted as Editors for the discussion document. Professor Christine Helliar is Professor of Treasury Management at the University of Dundee and the Institute's Director of Research. Professor Jan Bebbington is Professor of Accounting and Sustainable Development, University of St Andrews and a member of the Research Committee.

Part One

Chapter One

Introduction

Rationale for this report

This report investigates the pressures that accountants face in their working environment, and examines the challenging decisions that are taken which may affect an accountant's ability to maintain ethical standards. If the pressures on ethical decision making are identified and understood, then professional principles can be made to count, and the profession will be in a better position to enhance its image and maintain ethical standards. This report explores the ways in which these pressures can affect accountants and examines some potential remedies where action could be taken to help ensure that ethical standards are upheld. As such, this report aims to stimulate debate among a number of interested groups. Whilst the research surveys have drawn on the knowledge and experience of UK based professionals, the conclusions are believed to be of wider application.

The report has been written, in the year of the 150th anniversary of the founding organisations of The Institute of Chartered Accountants of Scotland, by its Research Committee. The reason for this focus is three fold. First, one of the hallmarks of professionalism has been maintaining high levels of ethical conduct in whatever working environment professionals finds themselves (Walker, 1991). An examination of the ethical standing of its members is, therefore, always an appropriate exercise for a professional body. Indeed, without the public esteem

Reference sources are listed in detail at the end of the report

that follows a commitment to such conduct, no profession can expect to remain strong and attract excellent recruits in the longer term.

Second, the role of accountants in the controversies associated with high profile cases such as Enron and WorldCom in the US, Parmalat in Italy and Polly Peck in the UK appear to have diminished the ethical standing of professional accountants in the eyes of the general public. While it can be argued that some accountants have demonstrated ethical behaviour in these well known scandals; for example, it was accountants who were the whistle-blowers in Enron, the image in the mind of the public is that the accountancy profession has been found lacking. This belief is part of a more general trend for the public to be sceptical of professionals, in general, and of the ability of all professionals to uphold ethical standards. Both of these forces have provided the impetus for the accountancy profession to consider its ethical performance and that of its members. This report thus reflects upon a more general concern about the extent to which accountants are 'taking ethics to heart'.

Third, it appears that the current business and commercial environment has placed an enormous pressure on accountants, wherever they work, which may result in decisions and judgements that compromise ethical standards. These pressures are documented by Zeff (2003) in the context of the American accounting profession, but the same trends are evident in the United Kingdom. There is no reason to expect that these commercial pressures on accountants will abate, and part of the accountancy profession's work in future years will be to (re)equip and support its members in a changing environment. Increased commercial pressures on accountants may be viewed by many within the profession as heralding a disquieting new era. Evidence of this disquiet is offered in Table 1.1.

Table 1.1: Disquiet with the current performance of accountants
The real question is whether audit and accountancy is a profession or a business. In the 1950s ours was a professional practice. It provided service for a fee ... Of course, our partners were keen to be successful. They did not want to lose clients to other firms. In their community they were respectable and well-to-do, but they were not rich. Neither would they compromise their principles ... Better lose a client than your integrity. This was a profession after all ... How different today. The big accounting firms have become vast, international and concentrated ... They are major businesses, with products and market shares, business solutions and profit performance as watchwords. Partners are judged by fee generation and growth ... Partner's rewards, though seldom published, reflect those of their 'fat cat' clients ... the real challenge lies in determining standards and living up to them, as it always did ... There is no going back to the profession of half a century ago. But I suspect that, unless auditing rediscovers what it means to be a profession and returns to its roots, state regulation of the audit process will have to be imposed to protect creditors, investors and the wider community. Last week I decided that the auditing profession I joined no longer exists, so I cancelled my membership of the Institute.
(Bob Tricker, explaining why he resigned from the ICAEW, *Accountancy*, June 2002.)

In outline, the remainder of this chapter describes how evidence has been gathered to address the aims of the research and describes the structure of the report.

Research questions

This report examines a number of questions that provided the original motivation for this study, and have been shaped and discussed at numerous meetings of the Research Committee of ICAS. The key questions addressed in this report are:

- Is there an ethical problem in the accountancy profession?
- If there is a problem, how pervasive is it?
- Is it more difficult for accountants to achieve sound ethical performance?
- How do accountants react to ethical dilemmas?

The research methods adopted and an outline of the way in which the data has been gathered is provided below. A more detailed explanation of the research methods and a reproduction of the research instruments that were used are included in Appendix One of the report.

Outline of research methods

A four-pronged approach to gathering data for this project was undertaken. First, ICAS sponsored three literature reviews on ethics. These examined: *Ethics and the Individual Professional* (McPhail, forthcoming), *Ethics in Business* (Lovell, forthcoming) and *Ethics and the Professional Accounting Firm* (Pierce, forthcoming). These surveys informed the design of the subsequent phases of the research and it is intended that they will be published separately as a report by ICAS.

Second, a series of in-depth interviews was undertaken in order to:

(i) discern the particular ethical challenges that accountants in practice and in business face; and

(ii) discuss possible ways in which ethical standards could be maintained.

While these interviews were primarily conducted with senior individuals within the accounting profession, they also encompassed accountants at all stages of their careers, including trainees, and covered accountants in a variety of work settings, in professional practice and in business. Interviews were also conducted with staff members of ICAS and the ICAEW as well as members of other professions, including a lawyer. In total 30 in-depth interviews were conducted and Table 1.2 summarises those who were interviewed.

Table 1.2: Interviewee summary

Interviewee category	Number of interviewees
ICAS employees	7
Big 4 employees/ex-employees (from partners to trainees)	8
Non Big 4 employees (from partners to trainees)	3
From other professional groups/other professional accounting bodies	5
Individuals in business	7

The interview phase of the project informed the third stage of the project, a postal questionnaire. The themes that emerged from the interviews were investigated in more depth in the questionnaires. The questions also focused on evaluating various proposals as to how ethical awareness and practices could be strengthened in the face of pressures on accountants. The questionnaire was distributed to a sample of 500 ICAS members of whom 157 responded. The completed questionnaires provided a more systematic and widespread view of how accountants viewed both the challenges with which they were confronted and the desirability of various courses of action that might be taken to obviate the possibility of ethical breaches. Table 1.3 summarises the characteristics of the respondents to the questionnaire survey.

Table 1.3: Summary of professional characteristics of respondents		
	Number	**Percentage**
Accountants in public practice (n = 86)[1]		
Position in organisation		
• Partner	44	51
• Manager	23	27
• Other qualified accountant	14	16
• Retired	5	6
Firm size		
• Sole practitioner	17	20
• 2-20 partners	32	37
• 21 + partners (non Big 4)	7	8
• Big 4	27	31
Years working in current organisation		
• Less than 1	4	5
• 1-5	26	30
• 6-10	16	19
• 11-15	15	17
• More than 15	22	26
Accountants in business (n = 77)[1]		
Position in organisation		
• Director	18	23
• Manager	32	42
• Other	12	16
• Retired	15	19
Company size by turnover		
• Less than £100 million	31	40
• £100-£500 Million	14	18
• £501 million - £1 billion	4	5
• More than £1 billion	25	32
Years working in current organisation		
• Less than 1	6	8
• 1-5	29	38
• 6-10	10	13
• 11-15	9	12
• More than 15	21	27

NOTE TO TABLE 1.3:

[1] Six of the 157 respondents filled in both parts of Section A indicating, perhaps, that they had recent experience in public practice although they were currently accountants in business. Not all of the respondents answered all parts of the question, hence the percentage totals for firm or company size and years working in current organisation do not sum to 100%.

Table 1.3 indicates that while the respondents worked in a variety of organisations and occupied a number of positions in organisational hierarchies, they tended to be at a senior level within the profession and business. This implies that the views expressed have been formed on the basis of many years experience in a number of work settings.

The final element throughout this project was to draw extensively on the combined professional and academic experience of a team of senior accountants on the Research Committee of ICAS. The views of this group, informed by the evidence that had emerged from the literature reviews, interviews and questionnaires, discussed and shaped the focus of this report.

Structure of the report

Elements from the various data-gathering methods employed in this research have been combined in order to investigate the two main themes emerging from the research. The research report divides into two parts. The first, encompassing chapters one, two and three, deals with the situations that accountants face in their working lives that may give rise to ethical considerations. In particular, how accountants recognise and conceptualise ethics, how they undertake ethical decision making, and the context and specific instances where accountants report that they have faced ethical challenges are described. This last task provides a flavour of the environment within which accountants find themselves and, therefore, provides an insight into the nature and scale of the challenges that the professional bodies face as they seek to support accountants in ethical decision making.

The second part of the research report, encompassing chapters four, five and six, focuses on the ways of improving supporting mechanisms that may enhance the ability of accountants to behave ethically in an increasingly difficult environment. It is proposed that action can be taken by the following parties:

(i) individuals, who are accountants, in the context of their personal development;

(ii) professional accounting firms as key players in the profession;

(iii) professional accountancy bodies such as The Institute of Chartered Accountants of Scotland;

(iv) other stakeholders such as universities offering accounting degrees;

(v) businesses that employ accountants; and

(vi) regulatory bodies that guide how the accounting profession and businesses operate.

Clearly, some of these parties are directly within the control of the profession, such as bodies that provide education and training programmes and set examination structures. Other parties require a partnership approach between themselves and the profession.

Chapter seven resummarises the recommendations in a format which allows linkage between those affected to be identified easily. It also highlights the finding that issues of ethical complexity tend to arise for indviduals at a particular time in their careers.

Summary

The purpose of this report is to examine the pressures that accountants face in their working environment, and to investigate the challenging decisions that accountants make that may affect their ability to maintain ethical standards. It is not intended that this report is produced as a 'snapshot' of current practice to be left to decay on accountants' shelves. The report identifies a number of issues and makes a series of recommendations that are intended to be the subject of reflection by individual accountants as well as those influencing policy in accountancy firms, businesses and institutions. Just as importantly, however, this work is intended to stimulate a process of reflection and change which will help accountants to behave in accordance with their professional obligations. There is no sign that the environment in which accountants work will suddenly ease or cease to provide numerous challenges that call for decisions to be made in accordance with high ethical standards. If anything, it is probable that these challenges will intensify. The nature of the ethical challenges currently facing accountants provides the starting point of this investigation.

Chapter Two

Ethics and Ethical Challenges for Accountants

Introduction

This chapter focuses specifically on what ethics means and outlines the ethical challenges that confront accountants. The chapter starts with a broad exposition of ethics and then narrows the focus onto ethical issues that accountants face in their working lives; whether working in a professional accounting firm, in a business organisation, or elsewhere. This approach has been taken because it became evident from the research that many of the ethical challenges that accountants faced were invisible by virtue of these challenges being an everyday, and less noticeable, occurrence, thus echoing the findings from Dunn *et al.* (2003). In some instances, this invisibility may have created the possibility that ethics *per se* is overlooked or is simply considered to be part of the 'usual' decision-making function of accountants. Thus, the heuristics, or rules of thumb, that accountants use to make decisions do not always have a recognised ethical dimension. Ethics, however, influences the behaviour of all accountants in all work settings and, arguably, accountants need to be re-sensitised to the existence of these ethical challenges in their work.

The research findings show that the majority of accountants who took part in this research intuitively understood ethics and articulated how ethics guided their decision making in their working environment. These ethical challenges, from a variety of sources, were pervasive in the lives of accountants, and the highest pressures derived from working relationships, business culture and the effects of competition. It was less clear how these pressures affected decision outcomes.

Defining ethics and ethical behaviour

Ethics is concerned with how an attitude, action or decision is determined as 'right or wrong or good or evil' (Donaldson, 1988). Such questions are timeless and have been debated by philosophers for centuries. Ethics has a practical application to any field of human activity. Accountants encounter ethics when deciding, for example, whether or not to:

(i) falsify an expense claim;

(ii) record overtime worked on an audit client even when it jeopardises meeting the budget;

(iii) sign an unqualified audit report when there is insufficient information to know whether the accounts show a true and fair view;

(iv) turn a 'blind eye' to irregularities in a client's tax affairs;

(v) manipulate figures such that financial accounts do not show a true and fair view; or

(vi) make people aware of conflicts of interest in business dealings.

Ethical decision making can thus emerge in a myriad of different ways in the life of a professional accountant. Some issues may be relatively trivial, even though there still may be a right and wrong course of action, while others may lead to severe consequences for all of those concerned, as various accounting scandals can testify.

Within the field of ethics, there are three possible ways in which an action or decision can be judged as right or wrong. These involve looking at:

(i) the consequences of action where the end justifies the means;

(ii) the motive for the action focusing on well-intentioned behaviour; or

(iii) the inherent 'rightness' of the action or doing the right thing.

More formally, these are described as consequentialism; motivism; and deontological grounds for assessment as summarised in Table 2.1, adapted from Gray *et al.* (1994).

Table 2.1: Approaches to ethical decisions

Approach	**Description**
1. Consequences	The consequences of an action are used to judge if the action was right or wrong. These consequences are often judged by the utility generated from the action – hence consequentialism is often characterised by utilitarianism. If the financial implications of an action are used to judge right from wrong, then a financial consequentialism approach is being used.
2. Motives	The motives of the person undertaking an action are the basis for evaluating the action. A good motivation with a bad outcome could, therefore, be ethically sound – although thought would have to be given to the degree of certainty that the desired, or expected, outcome would naturally arise from that action.
3. Right action (Deontological)	An action in itself is right or wrong. Many people, for example, would view murder as being wrong no matter what the consequences of taking a life, or the motive of the person involved in the killing.

Although unfamiliar with the terminology, individual accountants may self-consciously think in these terms when evaluating an appropriate action in situations that they encounter. Even if they do not consciously think in these ways, these ethical approaches are implicit in all decision choices. These different approaches can be usefully applied to The Institute of Chartered Accountants of Scotland's Guide to Professional Ethics, as given in Table 2.2[1], and the proposed International Federation of Accountants (IFAC) code, in Table 2.3.

Table 2.2: The Institute of Chartered Accountants of Scotland Professional Code of Conduct for Members
The primary duty of The Institute of Chartered Accountants of Scotland is to the public. This principle determines its status as a professional body, distinguishing it from the trade association whose sole concern is the interests of its members. A principal function of the Institute, therefore, is to ensure that the confidence in which the public holds the CA qualification continues to be justified. It is each member's duty and responsibility to observe high standards of professional conduct at all times. The gravity of this responsibility, particularly in recent years, is widely acknowledged and the Institute has therefore produced a comprehensive Guide for members to assist them in fulfilling their responsibilities as a CA.
Fundamental principles
1. You should behave with integrity in all professional and business relationships. Integrity implies not merely honesty but fair dealing and truthfulness.
2. You should strive for objectivity in all professional and business judgements. Objectivity is the state of mind which has regard to all considerations relevant to the task in hand but no other.
3. You should not accept or perform work which you are not competent to undertake unless you obtain such advice and assistance as will enable you competently to carry out the work.
4. You should carry out your professional work with due skill, care, diligence and expedition and with proper regard for the technical and professional standards expected of you as a member.
5. You should conduct yourself with courtesy and consideration towards all with whom you come into contact during the course of performing your work.

Table 2.3 IFAC Proposed Revised Code of Ethics for Professional Accountants

Fundamental Principles

(a) *Integrity*

A professional accountant should be straightforward and honest in all professional and business relationships.

(b) *Objectivity*

A professional accountant should not allow prejudice or bias, conflict of interest or undue influence of others to override professional or business judgements.

(c) *Professional Competence and Due Care*

A professional accountant has a continuing duty to maintain professional knowledge and skill at the level required to ensure that a client or employer receives the advantage of competent professional service based on current developments in practice, legislation and techniques. A professional accountant should act diligently and in accordance with applicable technical and professional standards in all professional and business relationships.

(d) *Confidentiality*

A professional accountant should respect the confidentiality of information acquired as a result of professional and business relationships and should not disclose any such information to third parties without proper and specific authority unless there is a legal or professional right or duty to disclose. Confidential information acquired as a result of professional and business relationships should not be used for the personal advantage of the professional accountant or third parties.

(e) *Professional Behaviour*

A professional accountant should comply with relevant laws and regulations and should avoid any action that discredits the profession.

Table 2.2 shows that the primary duty of ICAS is to the public. This has a consequentialist approach as accountants' actions can be judged by how they have impacted upon the public interest. For example, any action that is taken without due diligence or considerations of professional competence may have reputational and other consequences for the individual accountant, and the profession more generally. In the context of the accountant in practice, financial statements that do not show a true and fair view may have significant consequences for the operation of the capital markets. Indeed, one questionnaire respondent expressed their ethical duty as:

> *A responsibility to society, whose hopes and livelihoods depend upon honest and above board financial dealings.*

The Codes of Professional Conduct also require objectivity and integrity as fundamental principles, conflating the other two approaches by taking a motivist and "right" approach to ethical decision making. Mozier (1991) notes that "independence as an attitude of mind is only attainable for individuals who hold a deontological view of life, perceiving certain actions as morally obligatory, regardless of the consequences that may result from these actions". Thus, acting with independence, integrity and objectivity are intrinsically 'right actions'.

The above paragraphs illustrate how the professional codes of conduct reflect a range of ethical concerns and reflect all three approaches to ethical decision making; consequentialist, motivist and deontological. It is also implicit in the framing of the code that integrity is the primary ethical value of accountants, with the other values taking a secondary, but supporting, role. The *New Oxford Shorter English Dictionary* (1993) defines integrity thus: "Freedom from moral corruption, innocent, sinlessness, soundness of moral principle, the character of uncorrupted virtue, uprightness, honesty, sincerity". This view is consistent with accountants' own reported views of ethics in this study.

Accountants' views of ethics

In both the interviews and the questionnaire survey conducted for this research project, an open-ended question invited the respondents to state their definition of ethics. In the interviews, this question often appeared to take interviewees by surprise, and it occasionally took some time for a definition to be given. In the questionnaire, not all respondents offered a definition of ethics but a large majority, some 109 from 157 (69%), did so.

Definitions of ethics offered during the course of the interviews usually involved reference to:

(i) notions of "right and wrong";

(ii) "codes of behaviour", "frameworks" or "principles" that enabled decisions to be taken;

(iii) particular outcomes, for example, "not harming anyone"; or

(iv) specific ethical attributes that were particularly relevant to accountants.

In this last category interviewees responded to definitional questions by describing various ethical values, such as: "integrity, trust, honesty, fairness, responsibility"; and "adherence to professional rules, conduct, truthfulness, respect for others ... fairness". Many interviewees indicated that "integrity is ... the umbrella" covering all other aspects of ethical conduct or that "integrity is the roof that sits on the top of" other ethical elements. Indeed, one interviewee indicated that "integrity covers much of the other standards and certainly covers a guide to behaviour". Other interviewees broadened out their key ethical qualities in the following, typical, manner, saying that "objectivity, integrity and independence" were the principle ethical standards. Another stated that "confidentiality, integrity and objectivity … [are] absolutely critical".

These elements were also reflected by the questionnaire respondents who used much the same language to describe how they defined ethics. For example, the respondents offered the following descriptions:

> *Upholding the highest standard of integrity at all times, and being seen to do so, even if this results in internal or external conflicts, and having the confidence and conviction to continue to advocate an honest belief in the face of pressure to change a view or conclusion.* (Manager in a CA firm of 2-20 partners with 1-5 years experience in that firm)

> *To conduct work in a manner which will not damage the good reputation of the profession. Work in areas competent to practice in. To be courteous to all you come into contact with. To act with both integrity and objectivity in the interest of our clients without compromising the interest of the public as a whole. To make the right choice when difficult choices have to be made.* (Manager in a Big 4 firm with 1-5 years experience in that firm)

Notably, 25% of questionnaire respondents who offered a definition of ethics mentioned the word "integrity". Similarly, 22% mentioned honesty and 10% made reference to truthfulness. From the above review, the majority of accountants that were contacted in this project, and who offered definitions of ethics, defined ethics in ways that would accord with both a general definition of ethics and the overall philosophy of how ICAS and IFAC view ethics.

Not all accountants, however, had a readily available explanation of what ethics entailed. For example, some interviewees hesitated, or had to think for some time, before offering a definition of ethics, and a third of the questionnaire respondents did not offer a definition of ethics. Thus, for some accountants, ethics was not something that was well defined in their minds. Alternatively, these interviewees and questionnaire respondents might intuitively have known what ethics was, but had problems articulating it.

A number of the interviewees noted that they did not self-consciously think about ethics or about whether they were being ethical in their day-to-day lives. Interviewees suggested that ethical dilemmas were framed as "difficult business decisions" or "just part of the job which required judgement" rather than ethical choices. One interviewee noted that he had not talked about ethics with his peers while he had been a trainee accountant, but had talked about the challenges that he met in his job including aspects that, with hindsight, he described as being related to ethics.

It was also notable, with the exception of one questionnaire respondent, that the elements of the Professional Codes of Conduct were never quoted *verbatim*. It is notable that these elements, which have been designed to provide a framework for considering ethical issues, are being embodied in international codes, but do not appear to actively or self-consciously form part of the daily decision making of accountants. Indeed, a couple of interviewees referred to the existence of the Code of Conduct but could not recall its elements when they sought to define ethics. Further, one interviewee noted that, for him, the Code had not "been read in anger" – that is, actively consulted when contemplating a difficult decision. The Code, however, had been read for accounting training purposes. It thus appears that the Code may not be a 'live' document in the decision-making processes of accountants. Thus, it may be a desirable exercise to (re)engage individuals with the Code.

The above findings suggest that the core perceptions of ethics in the profession have endured, irrespective of the modern day challenges and pressures facing accountants. It appears that ethics remains an important consideration for accountants, even if not expressed in terms of the Code of Conduct or if ethical principles are not consciously thought about. Further, some interviewees suggested that the use of the word "ethics" or "ethical" might raise expectations that only a narrow set of issues were being considered, where right and wrong were clearly identifiable, and which fitted neatly within the scope of the ethical guidelines of the profession. In real-world situations, ethics addresses a wider range of situations than those covered by the codes.

Ethical challenges for accountants

Despite an inability of some interviewees and questionnaire respondents to be articulate about how they defined their ethical stance, the majority of accountants involved in this project indicated that they had encountered ethical challenges in their work. This section examines the context within which accountants' behaviour is, or should be, subject to scrutiny, as well as the types of dilemmas or challenges that accountants have to deal with in their professional lives.

The scope of ethical decision making

One area that was explored with the interviewees was the scope of professional ethics. Three ethical domains were identified in relation to the accountant as:

(i) a private individual (personal ethics);

(ii) a member of an organisation dealing with business issues that are not directly related to accounting activities (business ethics); and

(iii) a member undertaking a professional accounting role in a business or in an accounting practice (professional ethics).

It was often difficult for interviewees to make clear distinctions between how they thought about ethics in their personal, business and professional lives with a bare majority of interviewees seeing clear divisions between these different spheres. These interviewees considered that the scope of behaviour under each of the categories narrowed, from a broad perspective, in the personal and business arena, to a much narrower professional ethical stance. There was a sense that ethical standards were raised as this change of focus took place, with the scope of ethics being more constrained as the accountant moved through these three levels. A useful way of expressing this was offered by one interviewee who viewed these different ethical standards as being "interlockable, in that … there should be no difference … but professional ethics should be a much more developed set of ordinary ethics".

There was consensus that the Codes of Conduct applied both to members in practice and in business when they performed their accounting-related roles. This aspect has recently been discussed by the ICAEW, and Table 2.4 contains an illustrative case study of an ethical dilemma which a member in business could encounter.

Table 2.4: Illustrative case study of ethics as applied to members in business (from Bromell, 2004, p. 137-138).

Case outline

You are the Finance Director (FD) of an organisation. You become concerned that the Chief Executive is making frequent overseas trips and charging the expense to the organisation. The relevance of the destinations and the nature of the activities undertaken appear to have only partial relevance to your organisation's activities.

Your raise concerns with the Chief Executive, who gives assurances that the nature and purpose of these trips is covered by an 'understanding' with the organisation's Chairman. There is no evidence in writing, and no further justification for the expenses is forthcoming.

Key fundamental principles and duties

Integrity – Would processing the payment without an adequate explanation be seen as being honest and fair by others?

Objectivity – How will you be able to demonstrate your independence, actual or perceived, from the chief executive?

Performance – How can allowing the expense payments to be processed without adequate explanation be seen as acting with due skill, care and diligence?

Courtesy – How should you proceed so as not to discredit yourself?

An issue that concerned a number of interviewees was how the higher standards of professional ethics could be relaxed in what they perceived to be the less demanding context of the business domain. Several interviewees noted that it was more likely that tensions would emerge for accountants operating in business, especially in terms of defining what constituted behaviour that satisfied the criteria of integrity and objectivity in general business dealings as opposed to professional ethics.

In the interviews, questions were asked about the boundary between professional and other ethics. The interviewees were given a description of a situation where the financial controller knew that poor health and safety procedures operated in his company. The interviewees were asked whether the accountant should do anything about it, and whether professional ethics played a part in that decision. Interviewees agreed that health and safety concerns did not fall within the scope of accountants' duties, but that if there were clear and significant legal breaches then they should attend to the matter. Failure to deal with significant legal breaches would bring the profession into disrepute and, hence, would be seen to breach the Code. This was clearly a consequentialist view of ethics, rather than a 'doing the right thing' view and illustrated that rules, as enshrined in the Codes and statute law, were the minimum standard to which an accountant should adhere.

In this context the interviewees proposed other test-cases. For example, one interviewee asked a hypothetical question about an accountant working in a company that suffered an incident, such as the sinking of the *Herald of Free Enterprise* or the Piper Alpha oil platform disaster. If the accountant had known about the problem which had led to these disasters, but had not done anything about it, would that accountant have acted ethically? It was suggested by the interviewee that, while the situation that led to such a terrible outcome was beyond the scope of an accountant's professional conduct, its seriousness meant that it would be unethical to ignore it, regardless of how the content of the professional code was constructed. This was a further example of consequentialist reasoning, with the consequences being framed in terms of their impact upon the public interest.

Such stark examples muddied the distinction between general business ethics and professional ethics, and accountants who were not concerned with a situation just because it was not covered by a Code of Conduct were perceived as ducking the issue by some interviewees. The way in which the interviewees sought to support this position was to use the notion of 'acting with integrity' in all aspects of their work and personal life. Such a view fitted well with the notion of interlocking ethical standards which was noted earlier.

Thus, while Codes of Conduct only apply formally to accounting-related activities, where each code specifically states "work" or "professional," it may be that many accountants seek to adhere to higher ethical standards in other spheres of their professional and personal lives as well. Similarly, the standard of not doing things that would "bring the profession into disrepute" was a phrase often used by the interviewees and seemed to blur the distinction between the different spheres of ethical activity of an accountant. Thus, the demand to "ensure that the confidence in which the public holds the CA qualification continues to be justified", in the ICAS Code of Conduct, and this may also cover "not bringing the profession into disrepute". Other examples that were used by the interviewees to illustrate the difficulties of establishing clear boundaries between private and professional ethics related to handling stolen property and child abuse. Taking part in unethical personal activities demonstrated a lack of integrity and, because members of the public did not always make a distinction between the different spheres of behaviour of a professional, this would also bring the profession into disrepute.

The questionnaire did not directly address the issue of the boundaries between personal, business and professional standards of behaviour, but some insight could be found in the open-ended questions that were asked. Some respondents clearly believed that their actions were limited to their professional roles. For example:

> ***As far as professional ethics are concerned,*** *a definition would be that no member should behave in such a way, either in technical matters, or in their general dealings with their clientele, or other individuals or bodies, in such a way as to bring disrepute to the profession or to themselves* (emphasis added). (Partner in a CA firm of 2-20 partners with more than 15 years experience)

> *Carrying out our* ***professional*** *role properly. Being conscientious, thorough, having attention to detail, an enquiring mind and knowing what is right and what is not* (emphasis added). (Manager in a CA firm of 2-20 partners with less than 5 years experience in organisation)

Other interviewees linked their definitions to more than purely professional values. For example:

> *Acting as a professional, being courteous, seeking to do what is right, following proper rules and regulations, being fair and objective, carrying out work with care, upholding an image – all of this in business* ***and in your personal life too*** (emphasis added). (Sole practitioner who had recently set up his own practice).

> *High moral values such as: Corporate values of integrity, honesty, financial strength, quality of service, innovative leadership. Personal values of respect for self, truth, community, environment, future … and the ability to* ***combine these effectively*** (emphasis added). (Accountant in financial services company, turnover more than £1bn and 6-10 years experience in organisation).

> *Perform as a CA to best of my ability to ensure that my clients are advised properly on all accounting and legal matters affecting them. Ultimately, this is to ensure that clients also behave "ethically", by ensuring that myself and my firm behave professionally and responsibly.* (Accountant in a 2-20 partner practice with up to 5 years experience in organisation).

Another questionnaire respondent, when asked whether he had a clear ethical decision-making framework to resolve ethical issues, and if so, what the key elements of that framework were, responded:

> *Yes, I do have a framework. Very simply it is 'Do I consider this decision to be morally defensible? Do I believe that a reasonable man [sic] would draw the same conclusion? Will the decision potentially compromise my* ***personal and/or professional reputation?'*** *If the answer to any of these questions causes any doubt, then the decision is questionable and is therefore unethical* (emphasis added). (Accountant in an investment bank with 1-5 years experience in that company).

This quote, among others, suggests that, for some respondents, professional ethical standards are not narrowly focused on their actions as accountants. Thus, from this exposition of a framework, it appears that some individuals link their judgements to the public's expectations of accountants' performance as well as to professional and personal ethical frames.

The potential expansion of the accountant's role beyond a narrowly defined accounting focus is also echoed in the debate surrounding the future of the Operating and Financial Review (OFR). Some of the proposals for an amended OFR (DTI, 2004) focus on accounting data being supplemented with other relevant business data so that current and potential investors, as well as others who are interested in the performance of the firm, have a better base from which to make their assessments. Similarly, the new money laundering rules in the UK have increased the sphere of the accountant. The distinction between accounting information and other information is becoming blurred in much the same way as the interviewees suggested had occurred between professional and business ethics and their responsibilities in each arena.

However, the desire to separate ethical behaviour into distinct categories was viewed as inappropriate by some accountants in this project. Several interviewees noted that, even if there were different standards of behaviour, for them *personally* they did not use different levels of reasoning or apply standards of behaviour in these different spheres of their lives. One interviewee indicated that "a professional does not clock off at six o'clock and clock on at eight". Alternatively, there was support for the suggestion that accountants were not like "the police who are never off duty"[2] and that outside their professional area of expertise they did not have "a higher standard of care" than others.

The interlocking nature of personal, business and professional ethical standards appeared to be a common theme. Similarly, the scope of ethics appeared to narrow and the standards that were expected increased when moving from personal to business to professional ethics. It was also evident that individual accountants did not define their ethical stance independently from societal expectations. Indeed, such a relationship is clear from the Institute's Code of Conduct which notes that members have a primary duty of care to the public. As an individual's professional obligations are informed and conditioned by society, what constitutes ethical behaviour is likely to change over time, as distinct from definitions of core ethical values which do not change over time. In the same way, the ethical challenges facing accountants alter over time, and it is to these challenges that attention now turns.

Ethical challenges

An important aim of this project was to provide insights into what ethical challenges existed for accountants as accountants. The focus was not to document all the challenges confronted by accountants, but to identify the main challenges that arose and their pervasiveness. Two sources of information were developed. First, an open-ended question was asked of the interviewees about the ethical challenges that they had faced in the past. This question sometimes elicited 'stories' of situations, at other times it elicited a generic description of dilemmas that had been encountered. The second, and more systematic source of information, was gathered from the questionnaire which asked respondents to rate the extent to which various problems/pressures/situations/circumstances could lead to pressures that might result in unethical behaviour. Questionnaire respondents were asked to base their answers on their own direct experience and on situations that they had observed first hand. Both the interviews and questionnaire responses generated some interesting findings.

Many interviewees emphasised that the ethical challenges they faced were not of the "really immoral stuff like money laundering, insider dealing or outright fraud". Rather, most dilemmas and situations described by the interviewees invariably arose from their core business or professional practice and did not usually involve situations that were "blatantly right or wrong". However, having noted that very serious situations were not often raised by interviewees, a surprising number reported that they had been involved in potential whistle-blowing situations at some stage of their careers. These situations resolved themselves in a variety of ways, including, in one instance, the interviewee leaving the company and becoming unemployed.

One interviewee noted that ethical challenges often arose when someone was "seduced into the beginning of bad behaviour" in a context where the risk from that behaviour was not high. In one case this risk was gauged by the extent to which the judgement resulted in the accounts not showing a true and fair view. These involved "sliding judgements" that were acceptable one year because the judgement did not lead to a problem on materiality grounds, but became material, and thus unacceptable, in a subsequent year. By that time, however, the accounting treatment, or course of action, had already been 'approved' and thus changing course, or reversing that decision, was very difficult.

The outcome could then be an ethical breach, arising not as a result of a single decision at a particular point in time, but rather from the situation 'creeping up' on the accountant. In a similar vein, an interviewee in a training contract within business noted that he had experienced difficulty distinguishing between "is this just what business is like, or is this going too far?" Thus, it would appear that there is a danger of 'small' breaches leading to greater breaches because the situations within which choices are made tend to change. Paying attention to the possible longer-term consequences of current business decisions may assist in preventing more serious ethical situations arising in the future. Thus, when considering the appropriate accounting treatment for an item, the choice should be the same irrespective of whether the item is material or immaterial.

As might be expected, most interviewees had ethical stories to tell, indicating that accountants faced ethical challenges in their every-day working lives. In many instances these situations could have led to serious ethical breaches and several interviewees expressed the opinion that lasting damage had apparently been avoided due to luck rather than judgement. Indeed, two interviewees who were retired partners in different Big 4 firms, explicitly expressed relief that their past mis-judgements had not "come back to haunt me". These observations emphasise the need for 'good' processes to support ethical decision making within firms.

A sample of the dilemmas described by the interviewees has been categorised using the IFAC proposed code of ethics in Table 2.5. Examples of each type of ethical challenge have been drawn from the interviewees' personal stories.

Table 2.5: Typical ethical challenges

IFAC Code element	Examples of challenge in practice
Integrity	• Being interviewed and offered a job by a purchaser in the context of a corporate recovery client while working on the selling side. • Being sacked by a business for raising concerns over fraudulent pension fund management. The dismissal was framed as a difference in "management philosophy".
Objectivity	• Creating an environment so that accountants will leave in order to avoid having to pay redundancy costs, as an approach to human resource management in an accountancy practice. • Accepting the hospitality offered to accountants, accountants in business or in practice that: (i) inhibit independence; or (ii) is a form of bribe. • Facing the threat that a client will change audit firm if a set of accounts is not signed off. • Over-riding a more junior accountant's ethical decision purely to keep a client. • Loyalty to a client taking precedence over disclosure to the tax authorities.
Professional competence and due care	• Signing an unqualified audit report that should be qualified. • Preparing misleading financial statements in order to aid a client who is an acquirer in a take-over. • Presenting a rationale for an acquisition which does not reflect the true motive in order to enhance the perceived value of the acquiring company. • Dealing with breaches of legally required practices in the context of corporate recovery. • Manipulating accounting treatment in order to smooth income to the extent that the accounts do not show a true and fair view. • A conflict between keeping a client and recommending the correct course of action technically or legally. • Agreeing with an incorrect accounting treatment.

Table 2.5: Typical ethical challenges	
IFAC Code element	**Examples of challenge in practice**
Confidentiality	• Pressure to breach client confidentiality (such as disclosing information to a bank about the financial position of client) in order to secure corporate recovery work..
Professional behaviour	• Allowing expenses for tax purposes that are not business expenses and not reporting breaches of tax legislation to the appropriate authorities.

The questionnaires also sought to explore the reasons why, and how, ethical challenges, such as those outlined above, translated into ethical breaches. This focus was on personal factors, such as 'peer pressure to conform to current practice' and 'loyalty to a boss or to colleagues' which could lead to pressure to act unethically. The questionnaire also asked about business pressures, for example, whether 'auditors focused too much on chasing sales resulting in unethical behaviour' and whether the provision of non-audit services had increased unethical behaviour. The rationale behind the focus on these elements was to identify the challenges faced by accountants and to develop possible actions or remedies that could counteract the negative effect of these elements. These generic pressures on individuals, and a focus on the particular pressures that emerged in the context of professional practice, are examined separately in the next sections.

Experience of ethical challenges

The questionnaire gave respondents an option to indicate whether they had experienced a number of pressures that were suggested as increasing the possibility that an ethical breach would arise. An examination of the number of respondents who indicated that they had experienced such pressures enabled an estimate to be made of the pervasiveness of these pressures. Table 2.6 records the percentage of the 157 questionnaire respondents who stated that they had had personal experience of the pressures suggested.[3] However, the high percentage of respondents who reported that they had experienced these pressures did not necessarily mean that they made poor decisions as a result of these pressures. It is relevant to note that many of the respondents were senior members of the profession and hence would have had a range of experience to draw from in answering this question. As a result, it was not surprising that so many had come across these problems at least once.

Table 2.6: Experience of ethical challenges

Problem/Pressure/Situation encountered	% of respondents encountering this pressure[4]
Loyalty to a boss or to colleagues	88
Lack of personal confidence in being able to say "no"	87
Pressure from superiors	86
Peer pressure to conform to current practice	85
Pressure from clients or customers	82
Close relationships with clients/customers	82
A lack of a positive leadership or role model	82
Conflict of duties or interests	81
A commercial culture in a firm or business where results are more important than how they are achieved	80
A lack of financial independence hinders an independent view being taken	77
Personal greed or self interest may create unethical behaviour	74
Situations where the benefits on offer appear to be greater than the expected consequences of detection	67

Two observations can be drawn from this data. First, the most pervasive pressures relate to personal relationships with clients, superiors and peers. These are all conditioned by sociological processes within a professional's working life and are factors that can be influenced by institutions, such as ICAS, but are also pressures that can be resisted by individuals as well. Organisational culture is clearly an important influence on these sociological processes, and although it may be hard to change this culture, it is open to influence. In particular, initiatives or action that could be taken to strengthen the personal characteristics of accountants in these organisational cultures, such as their independence and integrity, are a necessary, but probably not a sufficient, precondition for counteracting the negative effect of the pressures listed above. Second, and in contrast, situations that are slightly less pervasive cannot be directly influenced by the actions of a professional body. Thus, the propensity for personal greed and self-interest are not as pervasive as the other influences noted in Table 2.6. These are factors, however, that some interviewees suggested drove unethical behaviour in the profession.

During the interviews, questions were asked about what would drive ethical performance, for example, the size of a firm, the client base or the geographic location. By and large, no clear patterns were discernible in the responses. Some interviewees believed that larger firms offered the possibility for more "checks and balances" to operate while others suggested that small practitioners were more likely to be ethical because their reputations were more easily made and lost in a local community. These contradictory responses might reflect the view that the 'grass is always greener on the other side'. One interviewee, who had worked for two Big 4 firms believed that "the two firms were identical in terms of their ethical outcomes, but that the processes were slightly different". Multi-disciplinary practices did not appear to create particular dangers, or at least, if they did, there were drivers that would make the maintenance of independence both easier and harder. The pattern of questionnaire responses supported the suggestions from the interviews that there were no defining organisational features that drove unethical behaviour in a straightforward manner.

Table 2.7 reports the perceived prevalence of the circumstances that might specifically affect individuals working in professional firms. Encouragingly, in all instances roughly half of the respondents indicated that they had no personal experience of these pressures affecting ethical behaviour. The commercial environment of professional firms did not seem to be as important as the personal and contextual factors surrounding the business environment, and reflected the findings in Table 2.6. The final column of Table 2.7 shows that many respondents did not think that any of these circumstances necessarily led to unethical behaviour. For example, only 27% agreed that interpreting standards for clients could lead to unethical behaviour. As accounting standards become more numerous and more complex, this is becoming an increasingly important part of firms' services. For example, the implementation of International Accounting Standards (IAS) and International Financial Reporting Standards (IFRS) in January 2005, has resulted in many firms advising their clients on the interpretation of these standards. Thus, it is encouraging that, based on their own experience, over two-thirds of the respondents did not consider this to be a problem.

Table 2.7: Circumstances which may increase unethical behaviour in professional accounting practices

Circumstance	Percentage of respondents who have had experience of this circumstance	Percentage of respondents agreeing or strongly agreeing with these statements
The increasing focus in firms on the need for commercial success to enable the income aspirations of partners and staff to be met has led to more unethical behaviour	56	42
The provision of non-audit services has increased unethical behaviour	56	40
Accounting standards have increased complexity which has increased the opportunity for unethical behaviour[5]	54	38
Interpreting standards for clients increases unethical behaviour	54	27
Auditors focus too much on chasing sales resulting in unethical behaviour	52	32
The increase in non-accountants in firms has adversely altered the ethical environment within firms	50	31

The highest ranked item by the respondents was the increasing focus on commercial success in firms where 42% of the respondents thought that the changing nature and ethos of firms could lead to ethical challenges. Although less than half the respondents thought that this was a problem, a number of the interviewees observed that the pressure on professional firms to operate as highly efficient businesses provided an environment that worked against the maintenance of high ethical standards. One manager of a Big 4 firm expressed the pressures thus:

> *I believe that the choice to make an ethical decision is within you … but when you are under work/fee pressure it gets overruled. You do not have the position or the space to say "hang on" … your career is on the line … I have seen it in one or two instances where someone has been prepared to stand up to the environment for what is right – these type of people tend to self select out of the promotion route.*

Another interviewee mentioned the disclosure of information to banks derived from reviews conducted on companies, clearly breaching client confidentiality, to increase the likelihood of winning work from the bank if the client was put into administration or receivership. This action was considered to be "good business practice" by the individual's superior, rather than being ethically problematic, which is how the individual viewed it. Further, one manager of a Big 4 firm suggested that:

> *Partners appear to bend the rules more than anyone else … I don't agree with this and I don't like it. I am on a fast-track to be a partner here … but I don't want to be a partner any more, primarily because I don't see how I can do the things that they appear to have to do.*

Overall a less positive picture of accountancy practices emerged from the interviews compared with the questionnaire survey. For example, the significance of these quotes reflects the literature on the ethical reasoning of accountants by Ponemon (1990), and supports the contention that ethical reasoning may decline with seniority in the organisation.

However, the questionnaire respondents, of whom 51% and 27% were, respectively, partners and managers, might have found ways of managing or resolving conflicts that were not observed by those who were more junior members in these firms, or their frame of reference for what constituted an ethical dilemma was different. It would be of concern, however, if the difference in assessment was due to senior accountants being less likely to recognise ethical dilemmas or less likely to be exercised by them. Unfortunately, this research did not provide enough data to be able to resolve this issue. Clearly the commercial environment of public accountancy practices is not likely to 'ease up' and specific remedies to reinforce ethical standards in this work environment may therefore be required. Chapter five focuses specifically on this issue.

In conclusion, in the context of undertaking accounting roles, there are a variety of ethical challenges that present themselves to accountants. These challenges encompass an array of situations, ranging from resolving conflicts of interest to ensuring that one's own self interest does not dominate a decision. Data from the interviews and questionnaire responses draws a varied picture, but it is clear that pressures exist and that they can translate into ethical breaches. While it is comforting to observe a diverse opinion and experience about the pervasiveness of the problem, there are many accountants who believe that ethical standards are being compromised. These findings suggest that ethics is an issue that needs to be addressed, and Part Two of the report focuses specifically on potential remedies to the shortcomings identified.

Summary

Situations that require ethical reasoning arise whenever there is a choice about a 'right' or 'wrong' course of action. Two elements need to be present in any ethical situation for an ethically 'right' outcome to emerge. First, the situation encountered has to be recognised as one where there is an ethical component. Second, the situation in which the decision is made, together with the personal qualities of the decision maker, should create a situation that supports the ethical outcome. The evidence in this chapter has provided information about each of these elements in the context of accountants performing their various professional roles. Specifically, an array of dilemmas has been identified from the interviews and these have covered issues that would be recognisable to most accountants. Many of these dilemmas have the potential for serious consequences. Often, the ethically appropriate response in a situation is entirely clear, for example, in a case of the breach of client confidentiality, but there is also evidence that even in these situations ethical standards are not always being maintained.

The diagnosis of how these situations arise, however, is less easy to discern from the data. There are a variety of pressures that appear to have the potential to both positively and negatively affect the ethical environment. From a positive point of view, many accountants believed that they had personal qualities, such as the confidence to say "no", which enabled them to maintain their ethical standards. Similarly, there were no specific organisational characteristics, such as size, that drove accountants towards unethical practices. On the negative side, however, commercial pressures from peers, superiors and clients to make unethical decisions had been experienced by some accountants.

The situations in which accountants find themselves are a function of the organisational and professional cultures within which they operate, the competitive environment where they work, the size or location of their organisation and the type of work that they undertake. However, culture and competition appeared to create the most pressure on ethical performance, but the extent to which these pressures translate into actual breaches are difficult to determine. There are challenges that need to be negotiated by accountants and chapter three seeks to identify the processes by which accountants seek to negotiate these challenges and make the "right" decisions.

ENDNOTES:

[1] The elements of the ICAS Code of Conduct are entirely consistent with other professional accountancy bodies. For example, the ICAEW's fundamental principles are: integrity, objectivity, competence, performance and courtesy.

[2] The money laundering legal requirements regarding a duty to report suspicious financial transactions suggests that, in this particular context, accountants are never 'off duty'.

[3] As is evident from appendix one, the questionnaire asked respondents to indicate "the extent to which you agree that the following situations can lead to pressures that may result in unethical behaviour, based on your **own experience** of such conflicts/pressures/problems in your own working life".

[4] Despite extensive testing of the questionnaire responses, there were very few statistically significant differences between the responses of the participants with different background characteristics such as length of experience or whether employed in a firm or in business. This suggests that there was a relatively large diversity of opinions on many aspects of the questionnaire. Statistically significant patterns of response are highlighted in the report where they emerge.

[5] The interviews and questionnaires were not framed in the context of UK accounting standards specifically.

Chapter Three

Making Ethical Decisions

Introduction

As outlined in chapter two, accountants are faced with a myriad of contexts within which they need to make decisions and take action. In many cases these decisions include judgements about what is 'right' and 'wrong'; that is, they involve ethical choices. Many decisions that accountants are involved in making have outcomes that will have an impact upon other parties. Thus, the accountant, knowingly or unknowingly, is making ethical choices all the time. For the most part, these choices are invisible to those outside the decision-making process. It is only when there is a breakdown in that process that unethical decision making and behaviour emerges in the public domain.

This chapter seeks to highlight these, often invisible, decision-making processes to consider whether they adequately address ethics. By providing an insight into how accountants think about their decision-making processes, it may be possible to strengthen their ability to make 'good' decisions in the face of the challenges outlined in chapter two.

The first part of this chapter draws on both the interviews and questionnaires to describe how ethical decisions appear to be made by the accountants involved in this research. Towards the end of the chapter, a conceptual picture is presented of how attitudes are formulated and how these translate into behaviour. This model characterises ethical decisions as being a function of culture and competitive pressures which were discussed in the last chapter and refers to the particular context within which accountants make decisions. The model outlines what accountants **should** do when faced with ethical choices and draws on material from the interviews and questionnaires. This information has been used by the Research Committee of ICAS to develop the final model which sensitises readers to what an ideal decision-making process should entail. The model has been used to structure the remainder of the report, in Part Two, on the interventions and remedies that could be made to strengthen individual decision making.

Modelling ethical decision making

Interviewees stressed that ethical decision making was the ability to make the "correct decision" and to not bring oneself, or the profession, into "disrepute". Ethical behaviour was based on being able "to tell someone what you did and not be challenged" or "not feeling embarrassed" by one's behaviour. For many interviewees making an ethical decision was a "gut feeling" and there was "a feeling of unease" when a decision was made that was unethical, rather than being something that had been carefully evaluated. Indeed, one questionnaire respondent referred to the "smell test" implying that a decision sometimes did not smell right (Retired partner, Big 4 firm). One interviewee noted that he realised that there was an ethical decision to be made when he found himself lying awake at night thinking about a client's problem, or thinking about a situation while on holiday.

To enhance ethical decision making and behaviour the various Institutes of Chartered Accountants in the UK and Ireland have provided guidance to their members on professional ethical matters for many years and the Chartered Accountants Joint Ethics Committee was established in 1991. Further, in November 2003, the UK Auditing Practices Board produced draft guidance on ethical standards for auditors and it is expected that this will be adopted in 2004. The elements from these guidance documents *should,* therefore, feature as significant factors in an individual accountant's decision-making processes, but as already noted in chapter two, this is not the case. Although some accountants clearly expect ethical decision-making processes to be "part and parcel of a well-structured PLC" (Director of a small recruitment firm), one finding of this study is that there is not a common approach by accountants to consider ethics in their decision making.

The interviews and questionnaires revealed a wide variety of ways in which accountants thought about ethical issues, and the way they ensured that the results of their decisions did not conflict with an ethical framework. These variations highlighted the difficulty of defining ethics in a way that could easily be applied to business and professional decision making and are explored further in the following section.

The findings suggest that there may be merit in the profession encouraging a more consistent approach to ethical decision making, particularly when professional disciplinary procedures focus on whether an individual has paid due regard to the principles laid down in the ethical guidelines of their Institute. At the same time, given the diversity of work environments and the complex decisions that accountants make, it is impossible to specify exactly how accountants should make all their decisions.

This study offers a simplified framework for decision making that is intended to address the apparent absence of a formal link between the profession's key principles and the practical application of those principles to practice and business situations, and so provide a consistent approach to ethical decision making. It may be that such a framework is already implicit in the decision processes of many accountants, but this was not reflected in the way that most respondents described their own thought processes.

One hundred and sixteen of the 157 respondents (74%) to the questionnaire provided more information about the key elements of their decision-making framework for resolving ethical issues, and supported the expectation that most accountants had thought about the ethical decision-making processes involved. Surprisingly, 27 of those who responded, indicated that they did not have a clear decision-making framework. For example, three questionnaire respondents noted that:

> *Unfortunately, no. Working for a small company gives little opportunity for a clear decision-making framework.* (Manager in a charity, turnover less than £100 million with 1-5 years experience in the organisation).

> *There is no clear framework for business issues.* (Retired accountant from a banking background).

> *No stated framework within the organisation for clear decision making.* (Manager in the retail motor trade, with turnover between £100 million-£500 million and 1–5 years experience in the organisation).

These contrast with the response quoted earlier that ethical decision-making processes were "part and parcel of a well structured PLC" and provide support for the development of a simplified framework for decision making.

A number of valuable themes emerged from reviewing the responses to the open-ended question in the questionnaire survey. The first explored the extent to which individuals used a set of *rules* to make decisions, or adopted instead a *principles-based* approach to guide their decision making. The distinction between these two approaches had been identified in the literature reviews, and the findings from this current study shed further light on this prior research. The second theme concerned the extent to which references were made to the *processes* that had been established to resolve dilemmas. The influence of peers was discussed in chapter two, and this is re-examined because a process-orientated approach could be introduced to strengthen individual decision making and to engage people jointly in making decisions. The third theme considered the extent to which *transparency* could be introduced into the decision-making process, and examined how consultation with other accountants could affect the ethical quality of difficult decisions. Finally, the extent to which ethics were seen to 'bite' at a particular *point in time* in accountants' careers, was examined. If a time could be pinpointed when ethical challenges were greatest for accountants then it might be possible to strengthen ethical decision making at this specific juncture. Before focusing on these particular aspects, it is useful to review how a sample of questionnaire respondents described how they made decisions.

Where a framework for ethical decision making was articulated, the following descriptions were typical of the responses gathered:

> *Is the proposed action legal? Is it honest and fair? Would I like someone to do this to me? How would I feel about this action being disclosed throughout the organisation or in public?* (Director of an oil industry company with turnover of less than £100 million with less than one years experience in that organisation.)

> *Moral behaviour which does not conflict with a modern interpretation of the Ten Commandments. Behaviour which is not illegal, except where it conflicts with moral behaviour above ... do unto others.* (Director in a life assurance firm with turnover of greater than £1 billion with more than 15 years experience in organisation.)

> *To do the right thing, am I required to lie about something, do I feel I can justify my actions?* (Accountant in business in an oil services company with turnover over £1 billion with more than 15 years experience in that organisation.)

> *It is intuitive and probably invoked only when breach is suspected. That is, I know something is wrong or dubious. Generally anything that results in an economic impact that is improper or wrong.* (Manager in banking firm with turnover greater than £1 billion and 1-5 years experience in organisation.)
>
> *The key thing is to do what you know is right and fair, regardless of how other people may view this. It is important not to focus purely on the short term. An overly short-term perspective may encourage unethical behaviour. By focusing on the medium to long-term ethical behaviour should be enhanced.* (Accountant in a local authority with 1-5 years experience in that organisation.)

These, and the other responses to the open-ended questions in the questionnaire, were analysed and the various approaches to decision making were categorised.

Decision-making approaches - rules *versus* principles

The first distinction that could be made was the extent to which the questionnaire respondents demonstrated a rules-based or principles-based approach to ethical decision making. A principles-based approach was usually described as one where some overriding criterion was used to make the decision. The use of the test of 'substance over form' or the pursuit of 'true and fair reporting' were often used as examples of a principles-based approach. In contrast, a rules-based approach to financial reporting focused on whether or not the accounting rules permitted, or prohibited, a particular accounting treatment. In the area of ethics, a rules-based approach could be used to evaluate objectivity, such as using a percentage of fees from one source to judge whether independence, and hence, objectivity was likely to be threatened. A principles-based approach, however, is more likely to evaluate whether an act or decision accorded with the concept of integrity or whether it could bring the profession into disrepute.

Bromell (2004) discusses this distinction and notes that while principles-based approaches appear to find favour, there are some reservations about their use. For example, he notes that regulators worry about this approach because "without a detailed list of prohibitions it is toothless and that detailed rules are easier and better" (p.131). Further, he notes that a principles-based approach requires "an awareness of potential issues, subjective judgement and the application of common sense in every circumstance where there might be a threat to adherence to the fundamental principles" (p.131). It is, therefore, possible to conclude that neither approach is fundamentally superior to the other, but that each has its strengths in application and enforcement.

However, the academic literature on ethical decision making suggests that in the US accountants tend to be rules-based in their approach to ethical decision making (Armstrong 1987; Ponemon 1990, 1992a and 1992b). The findings of these studies do not make comfortable reading for accountants. A rules-based approach to ethical decision making has resulted in a relatively unsophisticated state of reasoning by accountants, which is poorer than that of the educated population as a whole. Further, such an unsophisticated approach is assumed to be less likely to result in 'good' decisions because it is unsuited to more complex decision-making environments such as those experienced by accountants in real life. In addition, while age, length of experience and seniority in organisations appears to correlate with more sophisticated, and less rules-based, decision making in the general population, for the accounting profession a rules-based approach has been found to increase with seniority. Dunn *et al.* (2003) conducted a similar UK based study which supported the US findings, but with a less pronounced effect.

A systematic review of the questionnaire respondents' decision-making approach highlighted the extent to which a rules-based or principles-based framework was being used by accountants. Examples of responses that contrast a rules-based and a principles-based approach to decision making are contained in Table 3.1.

Table 3.1: Examples of descriptions of ethical decision-making frameworks

Rules-based approaches	Principles-based approaches
"Any issue has to conform to company policy, Institute standards, statutory obligations" (Manager of a construction firm, turnover between £501 million and £1 billion with experience of between 1–5 years in the organisation). "Use of ICAS guidelines" (Partner in CA firm with 2-20 partners, more than 15 years experience in that organisation). "I try to explain the legal position to clients and will refuse knowingly to act dishonestly" (Sole practitioner for more than 15 years).	"Yes, I do have a framework. Very simply it is 'Do I consider this decision to be morally defensible? Do I believe that a reasonable man would draw the same conclusion? Will the decision potentially compromise my personal and/or professional reputation?' If the answer to any of these questions causes any doubt, then the decision is questionable and is therefore unethical" (Manager in an investment banking company with turnover of less than £100 million with between 1–5 years experience in the organisation). "I always consider what action will lead to a true picture being known" (Manager in leisure industry company with turnover of between £100 and £500 million with 1–5 years experience in the company). "If I was a shareholder or financial backer would I be happy with the decision about to be taken?" (Director of a financial services firm, turnover of less than £100 million with more than 15 years experience in the organisation). "Personal integrity is the ultimate guiding force" (Manager of a facilities management firm with turnover of less than £100 million and between 1–5 years experience in the organisation).

These quotes illustrated the discrete approaches being taken to decision making, but there were also examples of respondents who used both rules-based and principles-based approaches together. Examples of a mixed approach included:

> *Intuition, reality, fairness, regard to law and regulation.* (Accountant in a 2-20 partner firm with 1–5 years experience in the firm).

> *Does this contravene any professional rules I am bound by. Does this offend my morals? If yes to either, decline what has been asked of me and explain why I will not carry out the task. If unsure, discuss with others, including the institute if appropriate.* (Manager of 2–20 partner firm with 11–15 years experience in the firm).

> *Is it legal, is it true, does it provide a fair picture, would I be happy to act on the picture provided.* (Director of a manufacturing and distribution company with turnover of less than £100 million with between 11–15 years experience in the company).

When the various approaches to decision making were classified according to a rules-based or principles-based orientation, it became evident that many questionnaire respondents were describing a variety of processes that they went through in order to make that decision. These processes are the subject of the next section.

The importance of processes to support decisions

A striking feature that emerged from the questionnaire responses was the extent to which both formal and informal processes were used to assist ethical decision making, and many of these often involved other people. The potential importance of involving colleagues in decision-making processes was evident from chapter two from the questionnaire respondents' ratings of the various circumstances that affected their propensity to behave ethically. In particular, the responses indicated that peers and superiors were perceived to have the potential to affect the decision making of accountants. If interaction with other people reinforces high ethical standards, then involving others in decision making is a potential feature to include in an ethical framework. However, if others have lower ethical standards then, conversely, *less* ethical decisions will result from consultation. Thus, using processes involving other people might be a double-edged sword. Table 3.2 outlines some examples of descriptions of decision-making processes that focus on involving others.

Table 3.2: Examples of a process-orientated approach to decision making
"Usually to weigh up the pros and cons of the situation, both for me and the company I work for. If I don't feel completely comfortable with the end decision, I will discuss it with my boss to see if I am missing anything or if he has anything to add". (Manager of a charity with turnover of less than £100 million with between 1–5 years experience in organisation).
"Consultation at all levels up to engagement partners and involvement of the independence of other partners". (Manager of a Big 4 firm with between 6–10 years experience in organisation).
"Planning stage - considered by partner and if potentially contentious the issue is reviewed by a second partner. During course of audit – technical issues discussed with compliance partner. Potential ethical issues subject to 2nd partner review and if sufficiently important formally raised in partners meeting for a decision". (Partner of a 2–20 partner firm).
"Consulting colleagues, consulting local compliance partners, consulting national compliance partners". (Manager of a Big 4 firm with greater than 15 years experience in organisation).

The processes described above varied in their degree of formality and involved individuals from both within, and outside, the firm where the individual worked. This focus on process highlighted the fact that ethical decision making often involved others in the determination of a final outcome. An important theme that emerged from the study was that consultation created transparency around the individual decision maker.

The importance of transparency

Transparency suggests that if individuals perceive that they are going to be held to account externally, they will think differently about a decision and, ultimately, may make a different choice from a decision that is not subject to outside scrutiny. Table 3.3 reproduces some examples of how questionnaire respondents viewed transparency.

Table 3.3: Decision-making frames and the role of transparency
"Understand the question, understand the circumstances in which the question is being posed. Consider against the background of this whether there are circumstances which could arise, where one's personal and professional judgement could be impaired. In looking at this if I was in a witness box would I be confident in defending it. In difficult cases, discuss position with a colleague familiar with the issue caused". (Partner, Big 4 firm with greater than 15 years experience in organisation).
"Considering the problem, in so far as you can, from the viewpoint of all parties involved, and then considering your decision on the premise that regulations, the courts, the public or even ICAS may question it". (Retired from International Private Banking firm with turnover of less than £100 million and more than 15 years experience in organisation).
"One test which can also be applied to aspects of risk management is to consider how something would look on the front page of the FT". (Manager of a Big 4 firm with between 6–10 years experience in organisation).
"Do I feel comfortable with what I am doing and if this ended up on the front page of the FT would I still be comfortable". (Qualified accountant in Big 4 firm with 1–5 years experience in organisation).
"I have two guiding thoughts - ten commandants is a good start and any subsequent self assessment is tested again. Would I be ashamed if my decisions or actions are subsequently published in *Glasgow Herald* front page". (Retired from chemical and mining company with turnover of greater than £1 billion having had more than 15 years experience in organisation).

Two observations can be made from an analysis of the above quotes. First, the importance of decisions being transparent *within* organisations was stressed by the individuals and suggested that either formal or informal mechanisms were in place by which internal transparency was achieved. Second, the possibility that those outside the organisation might oversee their decisions, and bring about external transparency, was also supported by the questionnaire respondents. Notably, ICAS and the newspapers were the most commonly mentioned external agency to provide this (notional) external assessment. Decisions that were visible to ICAS clearly introduced the possibility that 'wrong' decisions could result in disciplinary action being taken. Concern about visibility to the broader business community, through newspapers and other media, suggested that reputation, and the fear of disclosure, were also powerful influences for ensuring that ethically correct decisions were taken. Visibility and transparency are, therefore, necessary for sanctions to be applied to individuals who take an incorrect course of action.

Where ethics 'bites'

The final aspect that emerged as being relevant to the understanding of ethical decision making related to the stage in a career when difficult ethical decisions had to be taken. The point at which these decisions arise may dictate both the likely nature of those decisions as well as the potential consequences of taking the 'wrong' decision. Although the questionnaire respondents were not asked specifically about this, the interviewees offered their thoughts on ethics and career advancement. Several of the interviewees suggested that there were specific points in a career where 'ethics began to bite'. Several interviewees suggested that, within the professional firm, this point was on becoming a manager. A manager in a Big 4 firm expressed it thus:

> *The fulcrum of this process is at the manager level … if you are a manager in the Big 4 your eyes are on the next level and that is where the real pressure starts to bite … and the pressure is all about cost at this and more senior levels.*

Another interviewee noted that when he had worked in professional practice, ethics began to bite on becoming a partner, but he imagined that ethics now "bit" at the manager level due to the change of culture in firms to that of a performance-based emphasis. Similarly, an interviewee in business noted that the ethical issues arising from his accounting role centred on the Finance Director level, with ethical dilemmas focusing around the presentation of financial information. In addition, one set of interviews offered a view of accountants' decisions at three levels of seniority in a single firm: a trainee/near qualified accountant; a manager; and a partner. For this set of interviewees, the manager level was the point at which an awareness of ethical dilemmas became particularly evident.

The place, time and context of when and where ethics begins to "bite" has implications for the type of ethical issues that accountants are likely to encounter, the education and training programmes that are required, and other support services that may be necessary. From the above it is clear that a number of approaches can be taken in reviewing the decision-making processes of accountants, such as a rules-based and a principles-based approach. Further, the process by which decisions are made and the impact of the perceived transparency of the decision-making process are also important. A review of the ways in which these decision-making processes were described by the respondents was undertaken. These results are shown in Table 3.4. Often, more than one element was present, and in these cases the decision-making approach has been included under each category.

Table 3.4: Summary of decision-making approaches

Decision-making approach	Percentage of respondents illustrating some element of this approach
Rules-based approach	14
Principles-based approach	39
Process-orientated approach	39
Approach focused on transparency	8

This analysis suggested that the accountants in this study were primarily undertaking a principles-based approach to decision making, invoking a recognised process that usually involved other people. This approach is congruent with the approaches recommended by the various accountancy bodies and others, such as the Chartered Accountants Joint Ethics Committee[1]. Further, this finding is significant because it contrasts with the existing literature on decision making by accountants which infers that accountants' decision-making processes are poor because they are rule-driven (see, most recently, Dunn *et al.*, 2003). This variance with the results contained in the existing literature may have arisen because this current study asked accountants to self-report their decision-making frames, whereas other studies have sought to measure rules-based and principles-based behaviour on the basis of research instruments such as Rest's Defining Issues Test (1979, 1986). It appears, therefore, that the decision-making approaches most commonly described by accountants reflect those that the authors of this report would support, although such approaches are at odds with the existing literature in this field.

A generalised decision-making framework

The academic literature on attitude formation, and the translation of attitudes into behaviour, has been outlined in Table 3.5. This literature is based on numerous studies, completed over a number of years, which have sought to understand how humans behave in 'real-world' contexts. This generalised framework is used to describe what accountants **should** do in decision-making situations. The framework draws on the ethical guidance on decision making from various professional accountancy bodies and from the experience of making decisions in a complex environment.

Table 3.5: Translating attitudes into behaviour

Decision-making frame	Description of the phase	Explanation of the phase
Attitudes and social norms ↓ **Behavioural intentions**	Theory of reasoned action	"Behaviour can be predicted through measurement of the individuals' attitudes towards the behavioural action and social norms ... that influence the likelihood of performing behaviour". (Chaiken and Stangor, 1987, p.584).
Behavioural intentions ↓ **Behaviour**	Theory of planned behaviour	Perceived control has a significant effect on behaviour and is conditioned by volition control factors.

Table 3.5 focuses on the way in which behavioural intentions are translated into actions and, more importantly, identifies the extent to which other factors may condition these decisions. Two distinct phases of behavioural intentions connect attitudes to final behaviour. Behavioural intentions are formed by a mixture of: (i) the attitude towards something; and (ii) the social norms that exist about it. The attitudes of accountants, from the situations examined in this research report, have been formed from many sources, including education and training and prior experience. Good examples of formal social norms within the profession are the standards of behaviour identified in Tables 2.2 and 2.3, which reproduce the ethical codes of ICAS and IFAC respectively. At the same time there may also be informal, invisible social norms affecting attitudes that may either be in accordance with, or conflict with, formal professional norms.

The attitudes and social norms combine together to create behavioural intentions. The step between having an intention to behave and actual behaviour is controlled by "situational or internal obstacles to performing the behaviour" (Chaiken and Stangor, 1987, p.585). These factors are called volition control factors and may include, for example, the payoff from various courses of action or the organisational culture and control system of a firm. A useful finding of the behavioural literature, however, is that past behaviour is often the best predictor of future behaviour. Thus, if an accountant starts their career making ethically sound decisions, then there is a higher probability that they will continue to do so. Further, attitudes are invariably formed in accordance with social norms. This implies that if accountants are socialised into the profession in a way that emphasises ethical standards they are more likely to form attitudes that are congruent with sound decision making.

Many of those involved in this project stated that they did not have any standard framework for ethical decision making, but it was clear that they would welcome such a framework. The Research Committee of ICAS therefore gave careful thought to this and concluded that the generalised framework presented in Table 3.5 could be further developed in the specific context of accountancy practice. The resultant framework is presented in Diagram 3.1.

Diagram 3.1 A suggested ethical decision-making framework

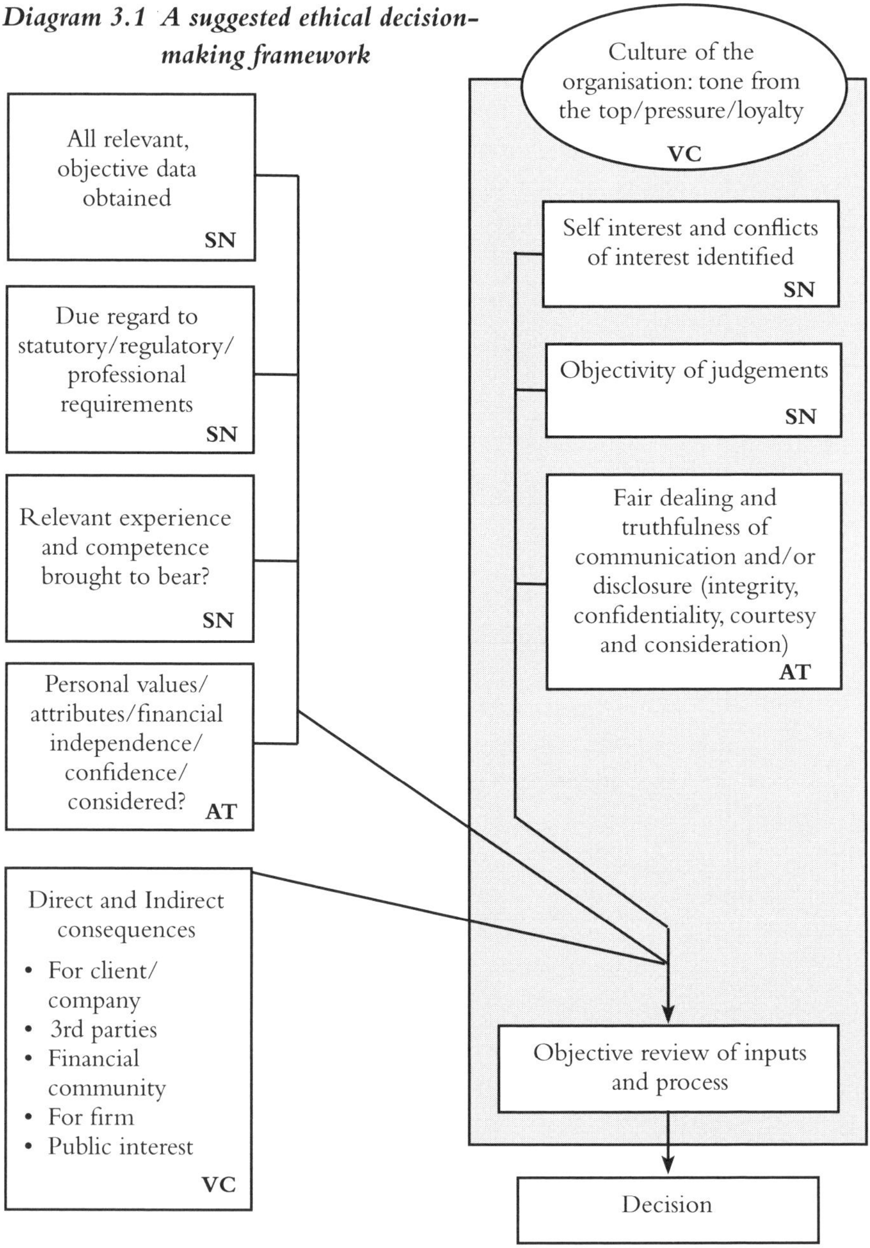

SN = Social Norms; AT = Attitudes; VC = Volition Controls

Diagram 3.1 draws together the principles contained in the ethical guidance for accountants. It describes how these principles should be brought to bear on ethical decision making. In addition, various volition control factors that will necessarily condition the decision-making process are included in the diagram, such as the culture of the organisation and the consequences of the decision. The model is intended to assist accounting practitioners and those in business to ensure that they have considered all the relevant factors, including their professional requirements, in a systematic way to improve communication and transparency. In the following chapters of this report, Diagram 3.1 will be referred to in the context of education and training and personal decision making as well as in the processes that firms and businesses could use to strengthen their decision-making approaches.

Summary

This project has examined the attitudes of accountants towards certain ethical issues using interviews and a questionnaire survey. In addition, the formal social norms of the profession and perceptions about informal social norms have been documented, and the extent to which behavioural intentions can be affected by volition control factors have been explored. The evidence suggests that accountants have both formal and informal approaches to incorporating ethical factors into decision making but that there does not appear to be a common approach. Some individuals adopt a principles-based approach, others a more rules-orientated focus but most decision makers use both rules and principles, together with a process, to reach a decision. These processes often involve other people, providing the opportunity for peer influence, which may have either a positive or negative effect on the decision made.

From the discussion in the first section of this report it is clear that the first three research questions identified in chapter one have become issues for the profession in recent years. Interviewees and questionnaire respondents acknowledge that the operating environment of accountants has changed, and will continue to do so, and that various elements of the new environment will challenge their ability to maintain ethical standards. It is unclear whether this anxiety has been created by change itself or whether it is a special challenge to maintaining ethical standards.

Elements of the changed nature of the operating environment have included:

(i) the increasing scale of business organisations, where problems could have a significant effect on employees, other organisations, the capital markets and ultimately the global economy;

(ii) a move from principles-based to rules-based accounting standards, introducing more scope for the manipulation of results and less reliance on substance over form;

(iii) a greater perceived distance between an individual's decision and the consequences of that decision, due in part, to changes in the scale of business and the Big 4 professional accountancy firms; and

(iv) a more litigious business environment which makes decision making more cautious and defensive.

The fourth, and final, question posed in chapter one refers to how accountants react to ethical dilemmas. There is no single approach to solving ethical dilemmas, as each situation, and the way accountants deal with each issue, is different. However, a generalised model of behaviour is presented in this chapter, together with a framework of how accountants **should** bring the various elements together to make ethical decisions. Part two of this report examines the remedies that individual accountants, firms and businesses and the professional accountancy bodies, such as ICAS, and other regulators could undertake to strengthen the likelihood that attitudes and behavioural intentions will translate into ethical decision making in the future.

ENDNOTE:

[1] The Chartered Accountants Joint Ethics Committee included representatives from ICAS, the ICAEW, and the ICAI. This Committee produced draft ethical guidance which was subsequently edited, approved and issued under their own badges by each of the Institutes involved.

Part Two

Chapter Four

Strengthening Ethics: The Individual Accountant, Education, Training and CPD

Introduction

As indicated in Part I, the research study drew extensively on the combined professional and academic experience of a team of senior accountants on the Research Committee of ICAS. The examination of:

(i) how accountants react to ethical dilemmas;

(ii) whether ethics are a problem in the accountancy profession; and

(iii) if so, how pervasive the problem is, would all be interesting in their own right.

Such an examination, however, would do nothing to help to change, or improve, the underlying situation. Hence, the Research Committee was keen to use the opportunities created by the interview and the questionnaire responses to explore a range of possible remedies to any perceived and real problems. In doing so, the Committee was alive to the risks of distorting the research process by leading respondents to predetermined positions. Care was therefore taken to frame questions in an open way and respondents were invited to make their own suggestions and comments on the issues in hand. Some potential remedies or suggestions were not supported by respondents, while others were, and in the next three chapters these responses are considered.

As indicated in chapter one, the combined views of the Research Committee, informed by the evidence that emerged from the literature reviews, interviews and questionnaires, are the focus of this report. The Committee considers that the results of this study lend strong support to some specific proposals and believes that they would justify further consideration by accountancy firms and institutes, businesses, and in some cases by other institutions, as well as by individual members.

The rationale implicit in this chapter is that professional accountants have a responsibility for ensuring that they maintain a competence to operate effectively. Maintaining competence includes being capable of dealing with ethical complexity throughout their career. There are two steps in ensuring ethical competence. The first is to make sure that prospective professional accountants have the background to achieve ethical competence on entering the profession, and testing this to ensure that it is the case. The second step is one where the individual actively plans and implements an approach to maintain this capability. Professional bodies should provide support to assist members to achieve these goals.

This chapter examines the impact of education and development across an individual's career as a professional accountant. First, the education of individuals, before they become professional accountants, is considered. In the UK this normally involves a university education, although only a minority pursue an accounting degree. In all countries, aspiring accountants need to pass the professional examinations and training curriculum of a professional body, such as ICAS. Second, all prospective professional accountants are also required to undertake a practical training component of three years, and the content of this is also considered in this chapter. Finally, in keeping with the theme of life-long learning all accountants have the obligation to undertake continuing professional development (CPD). Often this is achieved through a programme of training courses. Whilst this is perhaps the most obvious route by which to strengthen the professional values, ethics and attitudes of existing accountants, it is one which finds little favour with the questionnaire respondents. There are a number of other avenues that could be pursued by the profession to support individual accountants, for example through member services, and these are developed in chapter six.

The importance of education and training, and of embedding the resulting ethos within the organisation, was emphasised by one interviewee who noted that:

> *Enron had a fantastic* [ethical] *code, they did all best-practice things, but they never trained people, they never embedded the message and the leaders never did anything by example so it was exactly the wrong behaviour.*

Education and training for ethics, therefore, provides a powerful route to ensuring that ethical standards are embedded at the outset of an accountants' career and are maintained over their working lives. For example, in its strategic review "Fast Forward to 2010" (2003) ICAS stated that:

> *In the light of recent corporate collapses, and the resulting public scepticism towards professional ethics, it is appropriate that a major review is carried out on the approach to ethics education and assessment, both in the classroom, examination room and in the workplace.*

This review will be referred to later in this chapter.

Ethical education

The importance of ethical training was summarised by an accounting educator interviewee who stated that:

> *I see two purposes in an ethical education. One is that the person being educated can recognise an ethical situation when presented to them because the biggest problem with ethics is that people don't recognise situations that are ethical as ethical … and the second purpose is that having become aware of the ethical issue you need to provide a range of frameworks by which to take decisions.*

The grounding of ethics within education was emphasised by a questionnaire respondent who stated that:

> *we all like to believe that we meet the standards required through the fundamental principles … education is the key.* (Partner 2–20 partner firm).

Prospective professional accountants will have received, implicitly or explicitly, ethics education socialisation throughout their lives. Pre-tertiary education in the home, in the community and within formal educational settings will affect an individual's ethical stance, as well as the accounting education that is received leading up to qualifying as a professional accountant. The accountancy profession has no influence over an individual's educational experiences prior to university study, but as society, in general, is focused towards a profits culture, this may result in accountants having a profit-motivated view in their decision making. Indeed, one questionnaire respondent noted that:

> *In my opinion, people today are inclined to accept 'shades of grey' in their professional lives due to the increasingly dominant 'profits culture' of the Western World. Success is invariably judged by an assessment of short-term bottom line performance in isolation, rather than on a holistic basis.* (Manager, Investment Banking firm).

It is unrealistic to expect the accountancy profession to address or counter any such broad shifts in society. It is important, however, to note that this:

> *... performance-orientated culture, ... for businesses in general, and also for professional accounting firms and the public sector, in the guise of best-practice ...* [places] *... an expectation that performance, however, it is measured, should always be in the upper-quartile and certainly above the median ...* [and this thus creates] *... an impossible paradigm*

and one which may result more readily in ethical breaches (all these quotes from retired Big 4 partner).

General education

The International Federation of Accountants (IFAC) issued its first six International Education Standards (IESs) for professional accountants in October 2003. These Standards brought to the fore the need for accountancy educators, whether they be involved in pre-tertiary education, university education, or in professional education, to address thoroughly the requirement for education programmes to contain sufficient and rigorous content in professional values, attitudes and ethics. IES 3 "Professional Skills" mandates that "all professional education programmes should include some portion of general education". This general education is expanded to incorporate:

(i) an understanding of the flow of ideas and events in history, the different cultures in today's world and an international outlook;

(ii) a basic knowledge of human behaviour, a sense of the breadth of ideas, issues and contrasting economic, political and social forces in the world;

(iii) an awareness of professional and social values and the process of enquiry and judgement; and

(iv) experience in making value judgements.

This general education content is suitable for being incorporated into both the school curriculum and into many different parts of a university education programme, whether it is in an accounting degree or another degree. It is incumbent on all professional accounting bodies that they consider how to apply these principles somewhere in the early development of prospective professional accountants.

University and professional education

International Education Standard 4 "Professional Values, Ethics and Attitudes" goes further and specifies the coverage of professional accountancy programmes. In particular, attention is drawn to the requirement in IES 4 that:

The programme of professional accounting education should provide potential professional accountants with a framework of professional values, ethics and attitudes for exercising professional judgement and for acting in an ethical manner that is in the best interest of society and the profession.

The Standard continues by requiring that:

The coverage of values and ethics in education programmes for professional accountants should lead to a commitment to: (i) the public interest and sensitivity to social responsibilities; (ii) continual improvement in life long learning; (iii) reliability, responsibility, timeliness, courtesy and respect; and (iv) laws and regulations.

These are important targets for accounting educators to address and it is not clear that these are being achieved at present. Indeed, some interviewees who had recently, or were about to, qualify were asked if they recalled any ethics in their university education. One interviewee asserted that their degree had included "nothing [on ethics], and that is with a relevant degree" while another said that if "it was taught it was not memorable … I vaguely recall something in the audit course … I guess it would have been about independence". Yet another interviewee noted that "there must have been things in audit, but I can't recall anything … if any solutions were offered it would have been 'tell someone more senior about it'".

Although this was a small sample, it appears that ethics may not be given enough focus in accredited accounting degrees where, arguably, the curriculum requires a relatively large amount of technical detail to be taught. As such, some interaction between the profession and the universities that offer accredited degrees would be helpful, to ensure that ethics is not "falling through the cracks, or is not there at all, in university programmes" (Interviewee, retired partner, Big 4). For example, the profession could form partnerships with interested accounting educators to assist in the development of case materials which would enable ethics to be incorporated into courses in innovative ways. Indeed, a retired Big 4 partner interviewee suggested that the profession could help:

> *… to get people with on-the-ground experience involved in the teaching programmes … people with a clear idea of the tensions. It is my view that visiting professor posts are not used enough … most accountants are being trained at university by people who do not have experience of, and knowledge of, the business world. A practitioner would have the authority to talk about ethical challenges and how to deal, and importantly, not to deal with things. You could invite them to do this pro-bono … most senior people would be happy to give their time for this kind of role.*

The "Fast Forward to 2010" document from ICAS resulted in a thorough review[1] of its professional accountancy education programme and benchmarked its programme against those of other countries. Some third year students were interviewed as part of this review, and, in respect of ethics education at ICAS commented:

We didn't do enough. I can't remember much about it.

I can't remember if we did it in class or if it was home learning.

If it came up in an exam, I just relied on my gut feeling.

It's a wee extra bit they add in.

ICAS will shortly be implementing the recommendations from this research in the following ways:

(i) the introduction of a compulsory, short course in ethics and professionalism to be undertaken by all students at an early stage in their training;

(ii) the integration of ethics and professionalism throughout the technical subjects of the syllabus; and

(iii) a review, and improvement in quality control standards, of training firms to ensure that trainees are exposed to the application of professional values, ethics and attitudes in the workplace.

In addition ICAS will continue to provide courses offering further professional training for members in addressing and resolving ethical issues. The importance of such training is emphasised further, below.

The Research Committee's own interviews confirmed the need for action with regard to the content of ethical training that was provided to students. One interviewee noted:

> *My recollection is that it was poor … actually I can't remember anything about it at all really. That is how unimpressionable it was. Perhaps we had one day at TPE … I seem to recall thinking what was covered was very obvious.* (Recently qualified accountant, Big 4).

Similarly, another interviewee noted:

> *What I have done is read the guide to professional practice for the ICAS exam ... and so I know the key ethical aspects. I think there are five key things, which I can't recall now. Sorry, I can't bring them to mind.* (Trainee accountant, Big 4).

While the above two quotes paint a gloomy picture, it may well be that, for these individuals, ethics had yet to 'bite' in their working lives. Further, these interviewees did not suggest that ethics training should be abandoned in professional training. Rather, the issue was how best this aspect of accounting education could be tailored to meet professional ethical decision making. In contrast, however, one questionnaire respondent noted, without prompting, that:

> *I still find I draw heavily on my CA training, eight years ago ... I would encourage you to reinforce, and possibly extend, the ethical element as part of cases rather than discrete ethics studies.* (Manager, financial services).

Clearly for this individual, his accounting training had provided a good basis for his working life.

There was support for further professional training at the later stages of individuals' careers, not just from the professional bodies, but also from the firms that individuals worked for, and for the individuals themselves who wished to expand their own understanding and abilities. Continuing professional development is important because pre-qualification training alone cannot be relied upon to produce ethically sound accountants, and because the research shows clearly that it is not until an individual's career has advanced to the stage of manager or partner, or a senior manager or director, that the application of ethics becomes a major consideration in their everyday working lives. Hence, student training can only provide a sound foundation on which to add experience and on which to base a consideration of how ethical issues should be addressed. The decision-making framework suggested in Diagram 3.1 in chapter three is intended to provide, not only a foundation for the thought processes that can be used at the student level, but also as a mechanism whereby the different factors that need to be considered can be addressed in detail as an individual's career develops from training to practice.

Delivery and content

Whatever each professional Institute decides should be the requirements of their training qualifications for accountants, there remains a concern as to whether a classroom-based education is the best way in which to inculcate people in ethical issues. For example, interviewees noted that:

> *You can't teach people ethics, for example integrity and independence, … the best way to learn is as an apprentice, from watching people up the line. War stories are always very interesting to hear … it should not be a sermon, you have to work with it for people.* (Accounting educator).
>
> *Ethics can be taught … but I do wonder if people will want to be taught.* (Accounting educator).
>
> *It would have to be practical and related to real life and to work … but I appreciate that it is not easy to do that.* (Accounting trainee).
>
> *Case studies are alright … what we got my old partners to do is tell stories and talk about the issues that they dealt with to make it real.* (Accounting educator).

On the basis of these comments, some thought needs to be given to how best to introduce ethical issues into the curriculum and how to draw on the collective experience of accounting practitioners. The approach to the delivery of appropriate ethics education is currently the subject of an IFAC research project, supported by ICAS through the Scottish Chartered Accountants Trust for Education (SCATE), among others. The output of this research will lead to practical guidance for accounting educators, and is due to be issued in 2005.

The curriculum content of the professional accountancy bodies also needs active consideration. Table 4.1 reproduces the guidance issued by IFAC in IES 4 which specifies as a minimum the items that the curriculum should address. This is a powerful stimulus for the curriculum, and the research carried out for this current project confirms the importance of ethics in the curriculum.

Table 4.1: IES 4 minimum curriculum requirements
• the nature of ethics;
• the differences between rules-based or framework approaches to ethics, their advantages and drawbacks;
• compliance with the fundamental ethical principles of integrity, objectivity, commitment to professional competence and due care and confidentiality;
• professional behaviour and compliance with technical standards;
• concepts of independence, scepticism, accountability and public expectations;
• ethics and professional: social responsibility;
• ethics and the law;
• the consequences of unethical behaviour in an individual;
• ethics in relation to business and good corporate governance; and
• the ethics of an individual professional accountant, including whistle blowing, conflict of interest, ethical dilemmas and their resolution.

Two questions in the questionnaire directly addressed the issue of ethical accounting education, as shown in Table 4.2, which demonstrated that there was support for ethics education.

Table 4.2: Education and training related ways of reducing unethical behaviour	
	Percentage of respondents agreeing or strongly agreeing with these statements
Ethics should be examined in the professional exams – probably by the use of hypothetical scenarios	57
The education and training about ethics should be **increased** by the profession	53

The accountants in this study agreed that ethics should be part of the professional exams and that, certainly within ICAS, the education and training of ethics should be increased. The questionnaire respondents made comments that were supportive of the moves towards a more explicit examination of ethics. For example:

> *The Chartered Institute of Tax Professionals* [has] *rules and practice guidelines which are examined before membership can be achieved. These rules and guidelines are consistent with those expected of a chartered accountant. I would think it worth considering* [ethics] *as an examinable subject.* (Partner in 2–20 partner firm).

Another questionnaire respondent saw the potential for competitive advantage if ethics education was emphasised by, specifically, ICAS and suggested that:

> *The Institute must play a greater part in the monitoring and control of ethical standards in the profession. Standards in general are falling and ICAS must lead by example and have the courage to do so. Newly qualifieds do not have the training or receive the guidance necessary for high ethical performance. By leading in the field our*

qualification [CA] *will once more be seen as worthwhile.* (Partner, Big 4).

Other mechanisms for strengthening ethics through education and training were also suggested. For example, one interviewee believed that the inclusion of ethical criteria and benchmarks in trainee achievement logs and in the membership renewal process might provide a mechanism for strengthening ethical standards. Similarly, another interviewee suggested that, in line with the practice within his company, an ethics 'sign off' at membership renewal dates might provide a way of sensitising members to their ethical responsibilities.

The emphasis on ethics through membership routines did not, however, have widespread support from the questionnaire respondents. In particular, Table 4.3 demonstrated a lack of enthusiasm by the questionnaire respondents for these two potential approaches for reducing unethical behaviour.

Table 4.3: Education and training related ways of reducing unethical behaviour

	Percentage of respondents agreeing or strongly agreeing with these statements
All members of the profession should sign a "Hippocratic" type oath linked to the Professional Code of Conduct upon being admitted to membership for the first time.	46
All members of ICAS and other institutes should sign an annual certificate confirming that they have complied with the ethics code.	46

These findings were of concern, particularly when set against the research findings that it is not until individuals' careers have advanced to the stage of managers, partners or directors that the application of ethics becomes a major consideration in their everyday working lives. While it is impossible to infer why such approaches failed to find favour, it may be that these were seen as cumbersome ways of trying to create an environment where accountants were sensitised to ethical issues. This is considered further in chapter six. It could also be that the apparent absence of any common framework for identifying and resolving ethical issues may have made respondents dubious about whether such a procedure would have any real effect.

Continuing professional development

A more direct way to keep ethics in the forefront of the mind of accountants may be to incorporate ethics, and a suggested framework for addressing ethical issues, into continuing professional development in a way that ensures that members apply what they have learned in practice. Indeed, one interviewee noted that:

> *I find it hard to know what should be in ICAS training, or if it needs to be more, because I haven't seen anything in the job that has caused me to use my knowledge of what I have been taught.* (Trainee accountant, Big 4).

The inclusion of ethics into CPD is likely to be a useful way to support accountants' decision making, especially as the research suggests that this is when ethics begins to 'bite' in an individual's career.

> *You can't get to this behaviour* [ethical behaviour] *and deal with these pressures by only having ethics taught at the start of your professional life.* (Accounting Educator).

The ICAS strategy "Fast Forward to 2010" states that "ICAS will develop and move towards a system of compulsory CPD for all members which may include a core element of ethics awareness ..." This was confirmed in the review noted earlier which recommended that "ICAS should continue to offer and promote CPD courses that relate to ethics and professionalism".

This approach is consistent with the guidance given in IES 7 "Continuing Professional Development..." which states that:

> *CPD contributes to the competence of professional accountants and therefore acceptable CPD activities are expected to develop the professional knowledge, professional skills and professional values, ethics and attitudes of the professional accountant, relevant to their current and further work and professional responsibilities.*

This confirms that IFAC does not consider ethics to be a static knowledge-based subject but one that evolves and contributes to the life-long careers of professional accountants.

Traditionally CPD is used to ensure that accountants are kept up-to-date with new technical developments and other factors that will affect their professional activities. This is usually through input-based structured learning, often through professional and in-house courses. Thus, CPD can take place in the firm or business that employs accountants, through the profession, or from outside sources. All of these routes provide an opportunity to sensitise and educate accountants about their ethical responsibilities and to strengthen their ability to make ethical decisions.

The questionnaire respondents were asked three questions about CPD and these are reproduced in Table 4.4.

Table 4.4: CPD and ethical training	
	Percentage of respondents agreeing or strongly agreeing with these statements
Compulsory Continuing Professional Development training (CPD) on ethics should be introduced	32
Role play, cameos and case studies on ethics should be part of education and CPD	30
Members should be required to take self assessment tests as CPD on-line.	17

Tables 4.2 to 4.4 create a mixed picture of the questionnaire respondents' views. While incorporating ethics into education and training was viewed positively, in Table 4.2, there was less agreement that ethics training should be extended to the CPD environment. This lack of enthusiasm may reflect a general resistance to CPD rather than the dislike of post qualification training in ethics *per se,* or a reluctance for such training to be compulsory, or could reflect the doubts of respondents as to whether there was in fact any common framework for identifying and resolving ethical issues. In addition, Tables 4.3 and 4.4 show that there were reservations over administrative procedures such as sign-offs or self assessment tests for ethics although, again the reasons for this resistance were not entirely clear. Some respondents might have viewed the self-assessment tests as potentially becoming some form of ongoing examination that they would have to pass, and keep on passing. It is also possible that the respondents disliked an increase in the amount of 'red tape' that they would encounter, with little guarantee that a change in attitudes and behaviour would result.

Indeed, one interviewee noted that compulsory CPD training in ethics might impose inappropriate costs on all accountants when he stated:

> *I believe the profession is capable of self-regulation. The red-tape around ethics monitoring is in serious danger of becoming non-cost effective.* (Partner, Big 4).

The traditional view of input-based training courses as the predominant method of CPD is likely to be challenged by many professional bodies as they implement IES 7. Alternative approaches to ethical awareness might concentrate on the maintenance and achievement of competences where CPD is linked to personal development goals, peer review groups, team working, and projects. These innovative approaches could address the maintenance and development of professional values, ethics and attitudes in the same way they might address other more technically-orientated skills. As one questionnaire respondent stated:

> *I strongly believe that ethics should be instilled into one at the earliest stage of our career and then refreshed regularly,* ***tailored to the professional/business environment in which one works*** (emphasis added). (Partner, more than 20 partner firm).

Given the earlier suggestion, in chapter three, that ethics begins to bite at certain points in accountants' careers, it would appear that well-designed and focused CPD could be useful at a stage where more senior roles are undertaken. Such training and development need not necessarily be solely provided by the profession. Partnership opportunities between CA firms, businesses employing accountants, other relevant bodies, such as the Institute of Business Ethics and the profession could provide relevant and 'real-world' CPD offering intellectual and practical support for accountants when they require it. It is in the interest of both firms and individuals to explore ways of providing and obtaining good ethical training for individuals progressing up the career ladder.

Summary

In summary, a number of avenues that could be pursued with respect to ethical education have been identified. The interviewees and questionnaire respondents were positive about education and training for ethics, but there was less agreement about CPD, the most appropriate forms of post qualification training or the administrative procedures that could be adopted by the profession to encourage or monitor ethical awareness. However, a number of useful recommendations emerge from this chapter:

1. Insufficient ethical training is being provided at present. Action should be taken by the profession, accounting educators and academics to consider how, and in what form, ethics can be taught within education programmes.
2. Educational material that presents ethical dilemmas in a realistic manner and which are well designed for the task should be developed. Instances drawn from practical experience are of particular importance as this is not a subject that can be grasped easily by studying principles or rules alone.
3. Identifying and teaching an appropriate decision-making framework is an important element of ethical training, and such a framework has been a major contribution of this report.
4. Ethics should be examined during the qualification process. There is a need to consider carefully how best this can be done.
5. Firms and businesses should structure ethical training for all levels of seniority, not just trainees.

6. Accounting professionals should be sensitised to ethics in the work place, not just through pre-qualification and post-qualification courses.
7. Training should be designed to ensure that individuals recognise ethical issues when they arise, as well as how to address such situations.
8. Cost-effective and focused CPD should be offered to support accountants when ethics begins to 'bite' in their professional careers. That might well include the involvement of other relevant bodies.
9. Ethics should be linked to accountants' career development plans, team working and projects.

An interviewee from a professional accounting body (not ICAS) noted that:

> *We are focusing on how we communicate with members. How we can most effectively put that* [ethical] *information into the members' minds. Can we catch them early enough* [and] *how do we reinforce those issues?*

The solution is to start the ethics education process early and reinforce the message, as and when required, at key stages in accountants' careers.

This chapter has focused specifically on the action that can be taken at the level of the individual accountant. Accountants also have to work within organisations. The next chapter expands the exploration of ethics to examine the ways in which professional firms, and business organisations that employ accountants, can be part of the process of strengthening ethics in the profession.

ENDNOTE:

---

1 This report entitled *Student education in ethics and professionalism* was prepared by Diane Walters and others in 2004 for the Qualifications Board at ICAS. It is not publicly available but a draft copy was provided to the Research Committee.

Chapter Five

Strengthening Ethics: The Organisational Context

Introduction

The last chapter considered the ways in which accountants could be engaged individually in strengthening their pre-disposition to act in an ethical manner. Individuals, however, work within organisational environments and, as such, their action is shaped and moulded by these organisations. This chapter focuses on the ways in which organisational practices either support, or undermine, an individual's ability to make sound ethical choices. The interviewees in this study often saw themselves as relatively powerless to act in an ethical manner when the organisational dynamics did not support ethical behaviour. For example, one interviewee indicated that he was "not totally comfortable [with the practices] … but not so much that I would do anything about it" because it was not worth losing one's job over. Other interviewees also talked about situations where they, or others, had lost their jobs because they had spoken up for the ethically right course of action.

These observations suggest that strengthening an individual accountant's ability to recognise ethical issues and to choose the correct course of action, is a necessary, but not a sufficient, condition for ethical behaviour. Individual decision making had to be supported by the organisational setting. Accountants are employed in a wide variety of organisations and organisational influences will vary. The majority of interviewees recognised this, with an accountant in business interviewee stating:

> *I think ethics are influenced by your environment or what you are taught or what your management lay down for you so I guess, yes, it is quite possible for somebody's ethics to change over time.*

The three factors that are considered in this chapter on the organisational influence on ethics are:

(i) the way that organisations interact with their employees to strengthen or undermine the propensity for ethical decision making;

(ii) the issues that arise for professional accountancy firms; and

(iii) specific issues that affect accountants in business.

The recommendations that emerge from this chapter focus on how: (i) professional accountancy bodies, in partnership with employing organisations, can facilitate the sharing of knowledge, and (ii) organisational practices could strengthen the ethical culture. For example, the practical problems of implementating the expected "ethics partner" requirement of the Auditing Practices Board's ethical standards could be shared between firms to raise issues and concerns. Similarly, disseminating "best practice" may benefit the profession as a whole and the implementation of a framework for ethical decision making, as proposed in chapter three, could be used by organisations to strengthen ethical decision making.

Issues arising from the employment relationship

The employment relationship creates a situation where individuals are not always free to act as they may wish. Employers often ask employees to undertake certain tasks, and the employee is expected to carry out the request if it conforms to the employment contract.

However, employees may be asked to perform duties that are difficult. The interviewees in this study indicated that their employment relationships could place pressure on them. For example, when asked if the culture of a firm would affect ethical behaviour, a retired Big 4 partner interviewee stated:

> *Inevitably it does, partly because the culture of the firm has a say on who joins it. It is a soft, perpetuating thing that people tend to recruit in their own image and people are attracted to organisations that they perceive that they fit into, so that is a starting point. Also, the way the whole place is managed, and what is rewarded and what is punished, affects peoples' behaviours.*

Further, Table 2.5 demonstrates that a large majority of accountants involved in this project had experienced pressure to behave in ways that could have led to ethical breaches in their employment. For example, loyalty to a boss, pressure from superiors and peer pressure to conform to current practice were all encountered by over 80% of the questionnaire respondents. Table 5.1 summarises the questionnaire respondents' views on the steps that could be taken by employers to strengthen ethical behaviour.

Table 5.1: Employment related steps	
	Percentage of respondents agreeing or strongly agreeing with these statements
For professional accounting firms:	
Ethics should be part of a firm's training	81
The profession's ethical code of practice should be part of a firm's training	78
Firms should include assessment of ethical behaviour within criteria for promotion	59
Firms' recruitment processes should seek to assess ethical dimensions	56
For the accountant in business:	
The remuneration policies of companies should promote ethical behaviour	49
All companies should include assessment of ethical behaviour within criteria for promotion	49

Surprisingly, Table 5.1 highlights a split between the responses of those in professional accounting firms and those in business, with those in business disliking any organisational processes to recognise ethical decision making. The lower scores from those in business might reflect a perception that remuneration and promotion policies should incorporate far more factors than ethics. The professional firm respondents might have perceived a direct association between ethical values and core professional values, as noted by the Big 4 partner interviewee quoted on page 89.

Recruitment

Table 5.1 shows that there was support, from the questionnaire respondents, for recruitment processes to contain an ethical dimension. It is difficult, however, to suggest how this could be put into practice. Possible options could include psychometric testing, or the inclusion of ethical case studies at the point of recruitment, or the use of management evaluation techniques and group work. These options would be difficult because it assumes that: (i) a propensity for ethical behaviour could be determined in a straightforward manner; and (ii) it could be achieved cost effectively, which may not be the case, especially for small and medium-sized firms.

Interviewees also suggested that a formal evaluation process would not be easy to implement. For example, an accountant in business stated that: "I don't think we could measure ethics" and a member of another professional group noted that "no test for this [ethical ability] exists". Applicants for accounting traineeships probably have little knowledge of any framework for ethical decision making relevant to professional accountants, and thus recruitment based on an assessment of ethical decision-making ability is unlikely to be of general applicability. However, an interviewee in a professional body with Big 4 experience noted that:

> *If I were recruiting I would get into ethical issues with potential staff members to test their understanding of the issues.*

Thus, while some enquiry as to ethical awareness and moral standards are likely to be part of the recruitment process for professional firms and businesses, there is currently no uniform way to evaluate reliably any ethical pre-disposition. Therefore, from a practical point of view it is difficult to envisage a formal mechanism for including ethical aspects in recruitment. Rather, it may be that 'gut feeling' should continue to be used. For example, an interviewee, a partner in a Big 4 firm, when asked if he would recruit using an ethics focus noted that:

> *No. A lot of our people join us because, in fact, they are that type of person* [ethical] *anyway. They want to work in …* [an ethical firm] *and they see* [ethical standing] *… as incredibly important to themselves and so therefore if the firm is saying "this is what we do* [or] *aspire to" … that just encourages our existing staff and will be an attraction to others to say that* [ethics] *is really important for me and therefore I want to join this organisation.*

For this interviewee, potential employees did not self-consciously base their employment choice on their perceived ethical standing of a firm. Rather, ethical perceptions were inherently part of the organisational-personal match. This reinforced the perception that organisational cultures were important determinants of the ethical climate within which individual accountants worked.

Staff development

Once individuals become part of an organisation they become socialised to its norms and its culture. Over time, their experience in the organisation and their formal socialisation through training may affect their ethical standards. In professional firms the behaviour of senior partners is crucial, as this sets the 'tone from the top' and instils that culture throughout the whole firm. Partners should be seen to "walk the talk" and to demonstrate that the process matters and that the policies and procedures of the firm are important. Partners should also be willing to make pronouncements, both publicly and internally, to enforce the ethos that ethics matters and that the future success of the firm relies upon the ethical behaviour of its staff.

Observed standards of ethical performance are made when formal appraisals are undertaken or when promotions are made. The appraisal and promotion process itself could be used to assess ethics by requiring staff to self-disclose their ethical behaviour and to explain how they have managed ethics since their last appraisal. Further, ethics prizes could be introduced to publicly recognise staff who have made sound ethical decisions in particularly difficult circumstances. The interviewees themselves recognised the work pressures that existed which could counteract such appraisal and promotion criteria. For example, to be promoted within a professional accountancy practice it was essential that individuals met budgets, brought in income, impressed superiors, worked well with colleagues and were not seen to 'rock the boat'. There were, therefore, pressures to under-report the time spent on clients, to agree to requests from colleagues, and to portray themselves as people that 'fitted' into the firm. To 'rock the boat' with respect to ethics might disadvantage career advancement.

In contrast, sound ethical performance could plausibly lead to promotion, and other rewards, as part of a broader evaluation. For example, a partner of a Big 4 firm discussed the extent to which self-interest, in the form of desire for promotion, and ethical behaviour could be connected together. This interviewee noted that ethical behaviour on its own did not earn promotion, because ethical behaviour was presumed to be part of the job, but exceptional ethical performance, for example, maintaining ethics under considerable pressure, could be rewarded. In this context he suggested that:

> *I could see a situation where someone through their ethical behaviour has performed extremely well and provided the firm with an advantage and that could be recognised through a bonus, or whatever.*

The advantage that could be gained by ethical behaviour tended to be described as the avoidance of exposure to risk and, ultimately, litigation. The direct benefits from 'doing the right' thing were viewed as being less tangible, but real nevertheless.

Although Table 5.1 suggested that there was support for ethical considerations to be part of the promotion criteria for accountants, the interviewees were unclear about how to operationalise this ethical approach, especially without any generally accepted framework for ethical decision making. The framework suggested in chapter three may provide a solution to make such assessments effective.

This section has explored the extent to which employment-related factors could be changed to incorporate ethical issues. While there was support for such an approach conceptually, the respondents found it difficult to envisage how this would work in practice. The decision-making framework suggested in this report had not been devised when the interviews and questionnaires were conducted and, thus, the opportunity for discussion and transparency that such a framework offers was not explored with the respondents. The recommendations in this part of the report, therefore, are tentative in nature, and encourage organisations to explore ways in which they can assess individual awareness of ethical issues during the recruitment, training and promotion processes. Implicit in such a recommendation is the belief that a sound, ethical, organisational culture, applying a common decision-making framework, is the most practical way of achieving sound ethical outcomes. The following two sections use this general assessment of ethics within organisations to focus specifically on professional firms and business practices.

Professional firms

Professional firms have a number of clients and most have processes that reinforce high ethical standards with which to manage these client relationships. Professional firms also have management structures and a range of activities that they undertake, and these activities may affect ethical performance.

The questionnaire survey sought to examine the firm-client relationship, and asked respondents to indicate how much they agreed with a list of suggested remedies that could be introduced. Table 5.2 lists the remedies that accountants thought were important, and these are ranked in order, from those that commanded widespread support, to those that failed to find favour. Most of the respondents worked in a professional firm, but some members in business also completed this section.

Table 5.2: Firms' management practices designed to strengthen ethics	
	Percentage of respondents agreeing or strongly agreeing with these statements
All firms should introduce an escalation* process to help resolve ethical dilemmas (a process to report up the line)	76
Audit partners should not be able to make complex technical decisions without reference to technical staff	69
If a conflict exists within the firm, the technical partner or non-engagement partner should have dominance	64
Overall risk management responsibilities should be separated from business performance responsibility within the reporting structures of a firm	58
Each firm should have a reporting register or "incidents" book	45
A firm's code of conduct should be externally monitored	33
Firm's client acceptance procedures should be externally reviewed	27

* An escalation process refers to an arrangement within a firm through which ethical issues encountered by audit teams or individuals can be raised, discussed and resolved.

The issues covered by the remedies in Table 5.2 were also examined in the interviews, specifically under the guise of:

(i) escalation procedures;

(ii) the appointment of ethics partners and sign-off procedures;

(iii) firms as businesses, including the interaction between technical and engagement partners and the undertaking of non-audit services for audit clients; and

(iv) external monitoring and the local community.

First, however, the size of the firm is discussed as firm practices may vary depending upon their size.

Firm size and location factors

The potential for organisation size to affect the viability of various remedies for maintaining ethics was recognised. For example, a retired Big 4 partner, noted that:

> *There will be different remedies for* [firms at] *different ends of the spectrum because I think situations are quite different, and actually, they are quite a lot different between number four and number five because there is a big difference between the Big 4 and the ones below.*

Another Big 4 partner noted that:

> *I'd assume that in some ways you may not have the same infrastructure and bureaucracy* [in smaller firms] *but we need that* [formal structures] *because we've got several hundred partners. In a smaller partnership I'd suspect that first of all the partners must know each other very well, so I suspect there is a lot of trust between partners. I hope there is, and that they would deal with these issues almost across the table.*

In the same vein a small practitioner (Partner in 2-20 partner practice) stated that:

My own view is that the threat to the capital markets is driven by failures among the big accounting firms ... at the smaller end of the market there is not the same issue or the same effect from accountants' failure ... the effect is contained unless it is endemic to all accounting practices.

The ethics of even being a partner in a Big 4 practice was raised by one retired Big 4 partner:

Some people would argue that being a partner in a Big 4 firm is unethical because you earn so much money. I think it comes down in the end to individual behaviour and the way that you interact with society. If someone said to me, how can you earn what you do and think that you are being ethical, I would say, well, I've partly succeeded [in that I run] *an organisation that employs 15,000 people and I try to give them all a career structure and reward them well. We employ hundreds of graduates a year and train them and push them out into society. We try and give a service to the capital markets which ultimately is good for everybody and I work hard. Is that unethical?*

It was apparent from both the interviewees and from the questionnaire respondents that there was a belief that ethical standards were maintained because of a relatively high degree of transparency in the profession. This was especially so in a close community such as Scotland where those consistently breaching good ethical standards would be found out and the market would impose its own discipline, if the Institute did not do so first. Indeed, a qualified accountant in a Big 4 firm suggested that:

Reputation and image in Scotland matters ... Scotland is parochial in some ways ... there is a visibility about what you do and still some sense of old fashioned integrity in the system.

Further a partner in a small firm noted that "Aberdeen is a small village" and as such any poor practices by an accountancy firm would be known about quite quickly.

From the above, the size of a professional accountancy firm does not affect whether or not ethical standards are maintained, but the way in which standards are maintained might be different. For example, relationships between partners in a smaller firm may be more transparent, where partners can rely on interpersonal trust, than those in larger partnerships. Similarly, in smaller business communities, firms, regardless of size, would be subject to more informal scrutiny than would be the case in larger cities. The performance of Big 4 firms would also be likely to be more transparent by virtue of their size in any business community. Thus, although all firms are subject to scrutiny, the nature of that scrutiny may change according to the nature of the organisation and the business setting. Internal professional firm processes to ensure that standards are maintained may also vary according to firm size.

Escalation procedures, ethics partners and sign-off procedures

Both interview and questionnaire respondents viewed escalation processes positively. Escalation processes relied upon escalating problems to people who were capable of making the right decision and this led to discussions surrounding the role of ethics partners, to create a control environment which would maintain the standards of integrity, objectivity and independence, as enshrined in Codes of Conduct and the forthcoming Auditing Practices Board's (APB) ethical standards.

Hence the appointment of an ethics partner in accountancy practices with more than three partners is likely to become a requirement under the APB's ethical standards, making such an individual responsible for the adequacy of the firm's policies and procedures relating to ethical matters and the effectiveness of communication to partners and staff within the firm. The ethics partner is to be a senior partner, and have relevant experience and authority within the firm to undertake this task, as well as sufficient staff support and resources to do this job. The implementation of this requirement may be problematic for some firms in practice, and the professional accountancy bodies, in collaboration with firms, could facilitate the development and dissemination of best practice in this area.

The APB's proposed standards were in draft form during this project but interviewees were asked about the idea of having ethics partners. For example, a retired Big 4 partner with experience in business as well stated:

> *The idea of having an ethics partner is a very good one. It is helpful to have someone to be an extra sounding board with respect to how to balance keeping clients and making sound judgements. I have also worked for firms that have Major Client Advisory Boards ... that is a group of people who considered who were the critical clients. And they are not always the largest clients ... for example, the golf club could be a critical client because if you lost them due to your poor handling of the situation then lots of movers and shakers would know what problems you had and from that you would lose other clients. Such a panel would not be a blame culture thing ... rather they would be a community of partners that you could trust to mentor and advise on problem areas. When I did this sort of thing I always accepted problems at face value and then attempted to solve the problems.*

While there was support for an ethics partner by this interviewee, a partner in a Big 4 firm was less keen on the idea, stating:

> *Well I would hope that we wouldn't necessarily need to have an ethics partner because it is already part and parcel of our business.*

Yet another partner in a Big 4 firm noted:

> *I could perhaps see a situation where an ethics partner was there who was available for consultation with members of staff on a no names basis, just for someone who has something on their mind and they want to clear their conscience and take some advice. Or if a member of staff felt that the audit team were not getting to the right position and they had exhausted their avenues within their business unit to get there then, perhaps, it would be sensible for them to have recourse to an independent ethics partner. I think you have to differentiate between ethics and accounting technical issues.*

The above quotes highlight that some firms already have designated ethics partners and as a result already comply with the likely forthcoming requirements. Generally interviewees and questionnaire respondents were positive about designated ethics partners.

What failed to find favour, however, was increasing the amount of 'red tape' involved, for example, by requiring incidents records to be kept. Similarly, involving others in this process, and thereby further increasing its perceived bureaucracy, was disliked by respondents. Although some respondents clearly viewed incident records as bureaucratic and compliance-related, it may be desirable to have some knowledge of the extent to which individuals comply with ethical requirements. The presence of such records reinforces the ethical framework of the firm, may help to identify ethical breaches and help to suggest remedies and, thus, reduce the probability of future occurrences. As such, some record keeping seems to be essential, on a scale appropriate to the individual circumstances of the organisation involved.

The use of escalation procedures, incident records and ethics partners were not liked by all accountants in this study. For example, a Big 4 manager noted:

> *Sign-offs and declarations are not seen to be effective because you end up overloading senior managers with work. What you need to move towards is having people understanding and communicating sound*

ethical behaviour ... Sign-offs etc will be ineffective – bad practice will happen with sign-offs if you don't win hearts and minds.

Firms as businesses

The escalation procedures and culture of a firm may have changed over the last few years. Some concern was expressed by interviewees that accountancy firms were now run as businesses rather than as professional organisations. However, this change in emphasis was not purely for firms to pursue business goals, as a Big 4 partner explained:

I think you can be aggressive and still have a high regard to ethics ... do you push other people out of the way to get to where you want to be, well that is unethical. But you can still be a hard person and pursue an agenda but if you do it fairly and you communicate what you are doing to others and where you want to be ... .

However, a manager in a Big 4 firm recognised the tensions and stated that:

I have been in situations where some course of action/piece of advice is 'right', but given that it is not what the client wants your advice is overruled by those more senior to you. I believe that this happens because there are pressures at the more senior levels in professional firms. In particular, the culture of performance targets and the fee generation pressure creates incentives for bad/unethical decisions. It is very much if your fee income falls you will be out of a job.

The views expressed in this section suggest two possible remedies. First, it would be valuable to gain a systematic view of the historical way in which ethics partners and formal escalation processes have operated. Second, it would be instructive to review how various firms embed an ethics culture within their practices. Both of these may provide some value for other firms, especially smaller firms, by sharing their experiences of using these techniques. A clear decision-making framework to operationalise escalation procedures and incidents books might be expected to help considerably to ensure that an ethical culture was embedded within firms.

Monitoring

The interviewees were not enthusiastic about any outside monitoring of their practices. However, internal monitoring was viewed positively and was accepted as good practice. For example, with regard to client-acceptance procedures and engagement partners, a manager in a Big 4 firm noted:

> *There are also procedures in place for new clients to check that there are no conflicts of interest for audit partners, and various checks are undertaken in relation to partner performance. There is a process by which partners are graded according to their risk profile … if you get a five you are fine; if you get a one or a two your job is on the line unless the quality of your performance increases.*

Thus, beyond the changes in practice that affect all firms, there were no specific aspects which addressed how work routines were organised. What was apparent from the earlier part of this section, however, was the potential to support accountancy firms in their development of practice management routines to ensure that ethical concerns could be articulated and resolved. In this instance firm size might be an important variable. Large accountancy practices have the resources to introduce checks and balances in their practices. At the same time, control may be achieved in smaller organisations through less formal means. Thus, there may be a role for the accountancy profession to develop procedures that can be adopted in professional firms of all sizes, but which would be tailored differently for smaller and larger firms.

The accountant in business[1]

The cultural and working environment of a business is still widely perceived to be very different from that of a professional accounting firm even though, as noted earlier, firms are now being run more as businesses. As such, a number of additional factors may be relevant when considering how to support accountants in business. Indeed, a Big 4 interviewee commented that:

> *It is relatively easy to think about ethics in firms … but for me the real issues arise with accountants in industry where there are no other professionals around them for comfort. If in a firm you blow the whistle, others will back you up … if you do so in companies you just lose your job … even blowing the whistle to the Institute does them no good at all.*

Further, businesses employ people with many different professional backgrounds, different skills and abilities, and an accountant in an organisation may be the sole professional, or may be one of a small select group of professionals. In this environment it might be more difficult for an accountant to maintain an ethical stance in the face of diverse pressures. This could lead to a situation where, as an interviewee from another professional body noted:

> *Business members … find themselves isolated in the small end of the market. You will quite often find the member is the only member within the employer. So you can certainly sympathise with the idea that there is a lesser support network around a business member in that kind of environment.*

Thus, there is a threat, both in terms of isolation, and in maintaining independence. For example, an accountant in business noted:

> *I think … one of the difficulties of being all on my own* [is that there] *is no moral support at all, I have to make up my own mind*

> *about things and because I know the people very well and I hear their problems and that is what I meant about it not being straightforward to make an ethical decision.*

As for professional firms, the size of a business within which an accountant works may affect the changes and remedies that are faced. For example, the special challenges of working within a small organisation were stressed by an accountant in business who stated:

> *I don't think it depends on whether you are in practice or business, I think it depends on the size of your organisation and that is because of ... familiarity. When I was auditing we audited* [firm name and] ... *we were able to make very nice ethical judgements ... because we didn't know the people properly, we never saw them again. It was a huge organisation and it is quite easy to criticise it because it is a big organisation. Whereas now I'm in a small company I know all the people.*

An accountant in business in a larger firm mentioned differences in firm size, who stated that:

> *It's a lot easier for me ... when you have lots of people who you can ask and consult them so it makes it very easy whether you can go around and get opinions from people. If you are just one person on your own it is rather difficult ... maybe though the amount* [of problems] *are less large in a smaller organisation.*

To address these specific challenges faced by accountants in business, the questionnaire survey was sent to both accountants in practising firms as well as accountants in business. The business practitioners were given a different set of possible steps which could be taken to ensure that their ethical standards, when they were acting as accountants, were maintained. Table 5.3 lists the remedies that the respondents were given, ranked in order of importance. Some of these respondents worked in professional practice, but considered that they also had an opinion on these remedies, and their responses are also reported in Table 5.3.

Table 5.3: Business management practices designed to strengthen ethics	
	Percentage of respondents agreeing or strongly agreeing with these statements
Where internal audit exists, its review should extend to ethical issues	71
Audit committees should review ethical practices	70
All companies should have an ethical code of practice, clearly stated in their handbooks	62
If the finance director is also the company secretary, an independent director should be the repository of the incidents book	57
All companies should introduce an escalation process to help professionals resolve ethical dilemmas	55
A named person should be responsible for the escalation process and incidents book. This should be a board member (HR director/company secretary etc)	54
Each company should have a reporting register or "incidents book" maintained by a named person	39
A company's code of conduct should be externally monitored	28
Ethics officers should provide a system of formal consultations to their boards	24
All employers should require all employees to sign an annual ethics certificate	19
Ethical compliance should be certified by the Institute for Business Ethics or an independent body	17
Ethics officers should be appointed in all organisations	16

There appear to be three distinct groupings of responses in this table, ranging from those which command broad agreement to those which are not favoured. The first three set of practices are those which use existing control mechanisms to create and reinforce the ethical culture within an organisation and, with the exception of the involvement of internal audit, are those which are already contributing to an ethical culture. The second set of possible practices, which gained around 50% approval, are those which introduce more bureaucracy to the management of an ethical culture and may explain why these practices were not as favoured as the first grouping. It is, however, probable that all of these management practices are those which a well-run organisation already has in place.

The final six items in Table 5.3 were not well supported by the questionnaire respondents. The pattern of responses mirrored that in Table 5.2, where members in practice also disagreed with implementing similar mechanisms. These are all mechanisms which are likely to be perceived as being bureaucratic and, therefore, not meeting cost-benefit considerations. Similarly, the involvement of external parties in the operation of organisations was not favoured. Aspects of these remedies are discussed in more detail below.

Escalation procedures, ethics officers and sign-offs

Escalation procedure remedies for businesses echoed those for professional firms. For example, four of the nine factors in Table 5.3 related to escalation procedures, together with the maintenance of an incidents book. Respondents were very keen that an escalation process was established, and that there was a named person within the business that everyone knew that they could go to talk to about any issues. There was mild agreement that an incidents record should be set up, but this was not as strong as support for an incidents records within professional practices. A natural repository of the incidents record could be the company secretary. However, if the finance director was the company secretary too, there was support for the suggestion that the incidents book should then reside with an independent director.

The involvement of the Board was seen as a vital element of the process, and possibly reflected the Board's involvement in setting the 'tone from the top'. A director of a medium-sized travel business highlighted this point and stated that an essential feature was:

> *A clearly defined reporting line to the managing director, chairman and non executives. Attendance at audit committees also provides a forum to discuss issues outside of the normal board meetings.*

This was evidenced by the respondents' ranking the review of ethical practices by the audit committee as their second highest ranked item. Support for audit committee involvement was also demonstrated by a retired accountant from a large financial services firm:

> *Some suggestions may be fine in theory but in practice they may be too bureaucratic and impractical. The main approach should ensure that there is a visible 'escape plan' where individuals can go if they feel too much pressure to conform to an unethical principle. For accountants in business the internal escape route should be to the audit committee and if that fails, then the institute should be prepared to give support.*

The involvement of the audit committee was strengthened by its link to the highest ranked item; companies with internal audit departments should ensure that these departments also reviewed ethical practices. Thus, some form of accountability and transparency of ethical issues was rated highly by the respondents. This transparency was also supported by the third item, which stated that companies should have an ethical code of practice that was clearly stated in company handbooks. Interestingly, the accountants in business were against the idea of signing an annual ethics certificate. This appeared to contradict their preference for a transparent and accountable process.

Although there was no support for an annual ethics sign-off, it was interesting to note that one accountant in business, who had to do this for his organisation as a matter of course, noted that:

> *At the end of each year I have to read the organisation's code of ethics and sign-off to my immediate superior that I have complied with it. There are 40 specific questions which are asked in the form. I do find that I think about each element and reflect on things a bit. I don't know if it makes a difference, I haven't done anything in the list.*

Escalation procedures were generally well regarded, such as by an accountant in business who explained that:

> *There are within my own firm counselling services made available for those who have personal issues that they may wish to discuss and those personal issues may in part be derived from the workplace experience. So if you're feeling depressed and you think that your depression is due to the fact that your boss is not doing his/her stuff … . But that is something which is made available to employees and is done so on a completely anonymous basis etc, but it is there as a form of safety net.*

An example of how an escalation process worked was provided by an accountant in business:

> *Say it was being done within my area and I had the power then to change it then it would be easy. I'd be able to go in and change it. If it was done outside my area, which I didn't have any direct control over then the only route … I have got is to go to more senior management and make the thing public with them … or the other side of it would be to go to one of our regulating areas, one of our compliance areas or legal areas and discuss it with them.*

Monitoring and the code of conduct

Both the practitioners in business and in professional firms were asked about the external monitoring of their processes and procedures. There was clearly a dislike of any external monitoring. The notion that ethical compliance should be overseen by an external agency such as the Institute of Business Ethics was the second most disliked suggestion. The external approval of both firms' and businesses' codes of ethics did not receive much support either, with the former having very mild agreement, but the business members rejecting it outright.

One interviewee highlighted the extent to which accountants in business believed that the professions' code of conduct covered them in their business operations, and was similar to the discussion earlier in this report on the scope of behaviour covered by codes of conduct. A retired partner from a Big 4 firm believed that it would be valuable if it was reiterated that the code of conduct covered the accountant in practice and that it may be helpful if the code were modified or there was more guidance about the application of the code that reflected the dilemmas and issues faced by accountants in business. For one interviewee, however, it was clear that his professional status and the work he undertook within a business organisation were linked. Indeed, this finance director in a bank stated that:

> *I see my profession as being an accountant because, alright, I have worked for a bank for a long time but I've been doing accounting so I think everything in my role is geared towards accounting, certainly not banking. I don't regard myself as a banker.*

Summary

In summary, it appears that there are no particular obstacles to the ethical performance of accountants. Rather, it is the action of those working within organisational frameworks that dictate outcomes and the ethical tone that is set. Of the various remedies suggested, however, none were seen as "foolproof solutions" (Retired Big 4 partner).

The suggestions to improve ethical performance that have been reviewed in this chapter require a holistic approach to be taken. The 'tone from the top' of an organisation is a key component in ensuring that individuals within organisations operate in accordance with fundamental ethical principles. It is hard, however, for a single institute, such as ICAS, to influence the nature of the tone set by the senior members of its profession. Further, the 'tone from the top' is not sufficient if there are no processes that reinforce ethical standards. For example, a retired Big 4 partner noted that:

> *Leadership within whatever culture is crucial, supported by appropriate mechanisms … but mechanisms without leadership will not work.*

Specific recommendations which draw from the evidence in this chapter are as follows:

1. A decision-making framework, such as that suggested in chapter three, should be adopted by organisations to enforce ethical decision making.
2. The 'tone from the top' should be emphasised by key personnel through their actions and pronouncements to demonstrate support for individuals that take an ethical stance.
3. An ethical code of practice should be clearly stated in organisational handbooks.
4. Firms, and businesses that employ accountants, should make ethics a key feature of recruitment, training and performance evaluation criteria, using the above framework.
5. Appraisal and promotion processes should include self-assessments on ethics and reports on how ethics has been managed.

6. Organisations should consider whether it is practicable to introduce prizes or rewards for good ethical decision making.
7. Firms should establish escalation processes to help resolve ethical dilemmas.
8. Ethics partners and ethics officers should be established in organisations.
9. Firms and businesses should give active consideration to the introduction and maintenance of incidents books.
10. Professional institutes should facilitate a forum for experiences to be shared, such as the implementation of ethics partners, or ethics officers, in organisations or the dissemination of common incidents with appropriate remedies.
11. Professional institutes should facilitate the dissemination of 'best practice' especially as a valuable resource to smaller firms and businesses.
12. Within firms, procedures should be established to ensure that audit partners cannot make complex technical decisions without reference to technical staff, and that technical partners, or the non-engagement partner have dominance in situations where conflict exists.
13. Risk management responsibilities should be separated from business performance responsibilities within professional firms.
14. Audit committees should review the ethical practices of their business.
15. Internal audit departments should review ethical issues.
16. Professional codes of conduct should be written to reflect the work of members in business as well as those in professional firms and where such guidance already exists steps should be taken to publicise this.

This chapter has examined individual organisations. The next chapter continues to open out the frame of reference of the study and examines the regulatory and institutional framework within which accountants work.

ENDNOTE:

---

1 In the course of this research, the role of the accountant within the public sector has not been specifically examined. While many of the aspects noted here would be relevant to the public sector, not all will be, and there may also be specific public sector issues which arise.

Chapter Six

Strengthening Ethics: Institutional Factors

Introduction

Part Two of this research report, of which this chapter also forms a part, highlights the extent to which individuals' behaviours are conditioned by the environment within which they find themselves. The preceding chapter focused on how the workplace affected an individual's behaviour and the steps that could be taken to align sound ethical behaviour with organisational incentives. This chapter builds upon the previous one by examining the environment within which organisations themselves operate. The first section focuses on the interaction between the accounting profession and its members. The next section looks specifically at other ways to support accountants who are facing ethical pressures, in particular, situations where accountants possibly face losing their jobs because of their objections to what, in many instances, may be ethical breaches. The final section focuses on regulatory processes in financial accounting that could be used to enhance ethical practices.

This chapter concludes that there is scope to support accountants further, wherever they are working, through the services that are available to them as members of their professional body. Professional support by the Institutes includes providing information and counselling to those who seek it, as well as providing more practical support to those who risk losing their jobs through upholding ethical standards. This chapter also considers situations where accountants have fallen below the standards expected of them, focusing on a stronger and different disciplinary enforcement mechanism.

The interaction between the profession and its members

The questionnaire examined three changes that could be made by the accounting profession to increase the probability that its members acted in an ethically sound manner. The first of these focused on whether more support could be provided to members by the profession. The second change related to discipline and what should be done by the profession if ethical standards were breached. Finally, opinions were sought on how the code of conduct could be further strengthened so that it became a 'live' document and influenced members' working lives. It was noted by the interviewees that compliance with the code would help to resolve ethical problems but that the code itself should be examined to see if it were 'fit for the purpose'.

Member services

Table 6.1 provides a summary of questionnaire respondents' views on the various ways that ICAS, or indeed any professional body, could provide institutional support for their members.

Table 6.1: Member services enhancements

	Percentage of respondents agreeing or strongly agreeing with these statements
The existing informal and voluntary ICAS counselling service should advertise its services more effectively	62
The profession should seek to provide members with a mentor if requested	54
The profession should establish peer group or discussion groups	28
The profession should provide a discussion forum through the Institute of Business Ethics, or similar body	28

The ability to consult with, and to draw from, others' experience with regard to ethical concerns was considered to be a 'good thing' by the interviewees. For example, a retired accountant from a medium-sized organisation, noted that:

> *Close peers or supervisors posed the few minor ethical problems that I have faced. Those problems were resolved successfully by informal discussions with those same people. If I had needed a formal 'escalation' process due to an unsatisfactory resolution of the discussions, it would probably have to have been with that same group of people. I believe that formal help needs to be obtained from outside the business so as to be demonstrably impartial and independent and the Institute is the obvious source of confidential help for ICAS members in business. In addition, the width of experience obtained by Institute personnel across a range of industries will make the Institute's advice much more practical than the advice of someone who possibly just sees the ethical problems within one business.*

This interviewee clearly envisaged that his institute, ICAS, could provide an additional source of support for individuals.

Some ICAS interviewees did not appear to be aware of the fact that members could ring their institute and seek confidential advice on any ethical challenges that they faced. For example, one accountant in business noted that he was:

> *Not particularly aware of anything that the institute does. I sort of assume that they've got somebody I could speak to.*

Several other interviewees stated that they were not aware of any such services and, indeed, a retired accountant from a life assurance firm stated:

> *It is a sad reflection that these questions need to be asked. However, accepting that work needs to be done, I believe* ***a high profile consultation service*** *should be supplied by ICAS* (emphasis added).

While the above quotes suggest that there is a lack of awareness of existing member services, a partner in a small practice noted that:

> *Member services are unappreciated and under-utilised resources … I have picked up the phone to them … got a fast and authoritative response …* [these] *should be promoted more … the support is great.*

Indeed, the members services' consultation service within ICAS is used by members, although not very frequently, and is mainly used by the professional firms. The above suggests that a re-launch of this aspect of member services of ICAS could usefully be undertaken. Further, the provision of member services may be of greater benefit to those in smaller accountancy firms and members in business where it has been suggested that individuals may feel more isolated. For example, a manager in a Big 4 firm noted that:

If you went to ICAS for advice from a Big 4 firm you would be looked at askance ... there are internal processes to deal with this but if you were a smaller firm or a practitioner in business then I could see the value.

Similarly, there was agreement that providing a mentor, if requested, might also be helpful to members that were facing difficult choices, under the auspices of member services. For example, The Institute of Chartered Accountants in England and Wales (ICAEW) has a dedicated ethics advisory team who provide guidance by phone, email, fax or in writing. The ICAEW also has a substantial amount of ethics-related information on its website, including frequently asked questions and fact sheets. In addition, the September 2004 edition of *Accountancy* contains material which is specifically focused on supporting members in business. These are valuable initiatives which should be offered by all institutes.

The idea of providing a mentor also found favour with a retired Big 4 partner who suggested that one way to strengthen member services was:

Similar to the idea of a Major Client Advisory Board. It would be helpful to have a panel of expert people available to ICAS to informally mentor or advise people who needed it. I know that used to happen in the past but it has fallen off in recent years. It could be reinvigorated.

The interviewee viewed such mentoring as more than the help currently offered by Institute staff over the phone, and that it would be particularly helpful for individuals that were faced with a very difficult situation, and where the potential implications of making the 'wrong' choice were very significant.

While the availability of support services of Institutes were viewed positively, it is clear from Table 6.1 that any external involvement from outside the profession was disliked, even if that support was from an independent and non-political body such as the Institute of Business Ethics. Part of this reluctance to involve non-accountants in the affairs of accountants might have been the concern that non-accountants would not fully appreciate the subtleties and judgements involved in the accounting craft. It might also have been that accountants were concerned that they would unwittingly breach their confidentiality, or raise issues that their firms would prefer not to have discussed with outsiders. Nevertheless, it would be useful to investigate the extent to which outside expertise could be used to assist the profession in maintaining its ethical stance.

Some specific ways in which member services could be strengthened were suggested by individuals. For example, an interviewee from another professional institute revealed that it had:

> *A series of help-sheets that have been developed over the years to cover areas that appear to have recurring questions … a help-sheet that pulls out the points that you won't find in the handbook …* [from dealing with cases that had arisen] *through disciplinary cases.*

To communicate about members services, a member of another professional group with special responsibility for ethics suggested that the Institutes should use:

> *mouse mats, pens, mugs … the whole lot,* [in order] *to make people aware of how they can raise concerns.*

Thus, promoting a higher profile of members support services and the services that they offered would be valuable. In some instances, however, ethical standards will still not be met, and when this happens, disciplinary processes will need to come into play.

Discipline

Although the questionnaire did not directly ask questions about the adequacy of the disciplinary processes of the profession, some questionnaire respondents offered their comments in this area. For example, an experienced manager in a small firm noted that:

> *I would expect everyone admitted to a profession to have a high moral standard, but believe greed and self interest erode these standards. I would recommend the Institute to place more emphasis on punishing those who break the moral code and publicly disclose those who have been punished and in what way. External monitoring may allow us to punish those for minor breaches rather than wait till the individuals' ethics have disappeared completely.*

A retired accountant from a large electronics firm was more dissatisfied with disciplinary action and stated:

> *The abysmal decline in ethics is the fault of the various institutions who no longer seem to punish unethical conduct. No doubt the institutions have been pressured by the big firms, who pander shamelessly to major clients and who lead the way in promoting increasingly lower professional standards and ethical conduct.*

A manager in a small firm confirmed that:

> *I am 100% behind improving ethical behaviour. Regulation should come from the Institute, with severe penalties for those who break the rules. In my opinion it is the only way to regain the trust of the public.*

Indeed, the lack of severe penalties for misconduct, which invariably involved a breach of the Code of Conduct, were commented on by a member of another professional group with special responsibility for ethics:

> *To be honest, I think that the sums of money that you fine people are not the bit that is necessarily the deterrent for most members. For most members it's their reputation, having their name put in print, having done something inappropriate.*

It is difficult to evaluate systematically the incidence of different types of disciplinary action taken by the professional accountancy bodies, as there is no central repository of information. However, a review of some websites was undertaken, together with data for ICAS which was gathered specifically for this project, to gain an impression of the types of disciplinary cases that were being reported and the complaints that led to exclusion or expulsion from the profession. Table 6.2 summarises the types of complaints against accountants which were identified from the websites of ACCA, ICAI, CIMA, CIPFA, as well as actual data from ICAS. The ICAEW was not included in this information review because of the volume of complaints, reflecting the larger membership of that professional body.

Table 6.2: Complaints leading to disciplinary actions
1. Acting without proper authority
2. Bad work, unsatisfactory service/conduct
3. Criminal conviction/disqualification
4. Breach of company law
5. Change in professional appointment
6. Clients' money/fraud/dishonesty
7. Audit issues under ethical guidance
8. Failure to report to regulator
9. Conduct of liquidation
10. Delay/failure to respond (internal)
11. Judgement debts
12. Delay/failure to respond (external)
13. Fees disputes
14. Professional indemnity insurance issues

The complaints listed in Table 6.2 cover the last three years and they are ordered from the most to the least frequently cited disciplinary cases. The first three complaints made up half of all total complaints. However, two thirds of the most serious cases resulting in exclusion were for: criminal convictions/disqualification; acting without proper authority; and failure to report to a regulator. In the absence of more detailed examination of this data, a number of general points can be made.

First, as a whole there were a relatively small number of classifiable complaints and exclusions relative to the total number of accountants represented in the professional institutes examined; some 85 exclusions in total over approximately the last three years. The most frequent exclusions resulted from problems such as acting without authority or as a result of a criminal conviction, which might not necessarily have been accounting-related, although these complaints suggested that that there might have been some ethical failure of the members being sanctioned. In comparison, complaints and exclusions on the basis of poor quality work were relatively rare. The disciplinary action taken by professional accounting bodies should be made more transparent, and a summary of these complaints, for all the Institutes, should be made more widely available.

Revisiting the code of conduct

Another theme that arose from a number of questions focused on whether, and if so how, the form of ethical guidance provided by the Institute should be changed. Table 6.3 reports on two elements covered in the questionnaire survey.

Table 6.3: Forms of ethics guidance	
	Percentage of respondents agreeing or strongly agreeing with these statements
The code of conduct should be reviewed regularly	83
The principles of the profession's Code of Conduct should be given statutory recognition	52

There was clear agreement that the Code of Conduct should be reviewed regularly, but only a bare majority showed support for statutory recognition. Without statutory recognition, the enforcement of the Code over members facing disciplinary proceedings is potentially more difficult because individuals may be able to challenge disciplinary proceedings on the basis that they infringed their human rights. This problem arises from the Human Rights Act 1998 which can be used to argue that disciplinary proceedings infringe an individual's right to earn a livelihood. If the Code of Conduct became enforceable in statute, the human rights challenge would be eliminated, as it is for the lawyers' ethical code of conduct.

Making the Code of Conduct enforceable in statute, however, is not straightforward. Parliament would have to approve the contents of the code and this would not be without cost. Further, some interviewees saw statutory recognition as a double-edged sword. For example, a retired Big 4 partner stated:

> *I have reservations about making the code enforceable in statute … substance over form is important in all areas where there are 'softer' matters to attend to and ethics are soft matters … if you get things into statute then the lawyers will always fiddle with the words. If*

> *substance over form is a priority then you need to keep things out of a statutory code.*

Further, the same interviewee commented:

> *While I can see the argument that having statutory authority is helpful at the disciplinary committee … it is not that helpful. Once you are at the disciplinary committee you have lost it anyway … and the type of people who will employ lawyers and use the Human Rights Act to avoid disciplinary proceedings are the same people who would find ways around any form of ethics which are enshrined in a statutory code. So the code wouldn't fix the problem it was supposed to and may introduce a legalistic approach to ethics which would be counter productive.*

Thus, the debate over statutory recognition is a difficult one, and one that needs to be addressed by the profession.

Other support for ethical behaviour

Another difficult problem for the profession is that of how best to support members who find themselves in difficult situations that arise from ethical concerns. In the majority of organisations, consultation with colleagues and sound escalation processes are likely to result in ethical concerns being addressed and resolved without any recourse to outside bodies. In a relatively small number of instances, however, internal resolution processes will not result in an ethical outcome. In these instances the choices available to an individual may be relatively limited. Often, there may only be two choices available: to lose their job, or 'whistle blow'.

This section considers these rarer instances where there may be a need for further support for individuals because the outcome of making the correct decision from an ethical standpoint may mean that their jobs, and livelihoods, are on the line. Table 6.4 presents the questionnaire respondents' views on the help that ICAS could give to those individuals who found themselves in difficult situations because of their ethical choices.

Table 6.4: Further support for ethical decision making	
	Percentage of respondents agreeing or strongly agreeing with these statements
Members consulting the service* and subsequently losing their jobs could state on their *CV* that they had consulted and that ICAS retained a record of the matter(s) covered and the relevant date(s)	69
ICAS should provide an in-house service to potential whistle-blowers even if membership fees had to increase	46
ICAS should provide an independent external service to potential whistle-blowers even if membership fees increased	38
ICAS should offer an insurance service to members for losing a job through whistle-blowing even if membership fees increased	28

* In the questionnaire, the service was described as an in-house service provided by ICAS to support members who found themselves in a potential whistle-blowing situation.

As is evident from the above Table, there is a large gap between the top ranking item and the other items listed. There was a great deal of support for a formal process whereby someone who was facing a difficult situation should be supported by the Institute to make an ethical decision. The 'service' offered would provide formal documentation of situations where members of ICAS, or other bodies, feared for their jobs because they maintained their ethical standards. If the individual subsequently lost their job, and as a result was unable to obtain a reference from their previous employer, then their Institute could vouch that they had discussed an ethical issue and taken advice. Such a service would help to remove the stigma that is sometimes attached to an individual who has 'whistle blown' and may encourage individuals, who are at risk of losing their jobs, to hold their ethical line.

Clearly, there is a risk that such a service might be the subject of abuse. For example, some individuals may act improperly and know that they are about to be dismissed and could use this service to make it look as if they had been the victims. However, such a risk could be addressed by the careful application of enquiry procedures by the member's institute. Further, employers who consider that some accountants have acted improperly or dishonestly could notify the offending members' professional bodies, and this could be taken into account when these members request the attestation that it had been consulted.

Agreement with other remedies in Table 6.4 had less support. For example, just under half of the questionnaire respondents agreed that ICAS should provide services to whistle-blowers. The questions in this area were conditional on membership fees increasing and it may be that respondents were keen on the service, but not at an increased cost to themselves. Indeed, an experienced sole practitioner ventured that:

> *ICAS should perhaps offer an insurance scheme to members losing their job through whistle blowing, but at their own expense and not through increased membership fees.*

It may also have been that respondents recognised that there was an existing statutory support framework for whistle blowers, and therefore, ICAS did not need to devote further resources.

There is merit in supporting members who exercise sound ethical judgements but who subsequently lose their jobs. It is difficult to gauge how frequently accountants lose their jobs because of their professional integrity, but it was instructive that a number of the interviewees provided stories of this type. For example, when asked about ethical dilemmas, an accountant in business noted:

> *Well I suppose one of the major ones is that I was being asked to be economical with the truth as a finance director and in the end I refused to do it and voted with my feet.*

In another instance, a partner in a Big 4 firm had also been in this situation earlier in his career, not long after qualifying. His story is briefly retold below as it is illustrative of the pressures that emerge in such a situation.

> *When I qualified … I had a couple of jobs in commerce and then took a job as group financial controller of a publicly listed group, who better remain nameless. I hadn't been there very long when the company secretary said 'you'd better have a look at the pension fund because I'm not happy with the way it's being run'. To cut a long story short, the group were collecting the contributions from employees for the pension fund but for about 12 months or so hadn't paid over any of the contributions into the fund. So I looked into this and approached the group finance director and said this clearly wasn't right and his response was that the accounting is such a mess that we just don't know how much the fund is due in respect of employee contributions so sort it out and regularise the situation. So I did that and came up with a sum* [of a material amount] *… so I said presumably now we can pay this into the pension fund and his response then was we think the fund is probably over-funded so there is no point because we'd just get it back anyway. Which was a moot point because taking money out of a pension fund is not that easy, can't just say its over-funded and therefore we don't have to pay*

it over. So at that point I was still fairly newly qualified to be honest and wasn't quite sure where to go but I found … an ethics advisory [service] … *for members in industry where they could take advice as for their professional position on matters. They put me in touch with* [someone] … *an industry expert and I took him through the facts I've just stated. I always remember his response was well this is clearly unethical, it's wrong and you must record your concerns in writing and then he said you'll probably get the sack. So I thanked him for that advice and it was clear what I had to do and I did that at which point I think I wrote a letter to the chairman who was also the chief executive at the time, of this group. Although they would swear there was no direct link, the next day I got the sack. I'd only been there less than six months so contractually they were able to give me a day's notice, in fact they gave me a month's notice and paid me for a further month but I was asked to clear my desk that day. I said is this anything to do with the pension funds issue and they said not at all and we just believe that our management philosophy are somewhat different in this, a relationship that is not going to work. So I left that day, I thought about what I should do further and I thought the only thing I could do was talk to the auditors at the time who were quite a well-known firm. I don't know what they did after that because obviously I wasn't around to see, but I'm afraid I got the clear impression from them that they didn't have the appetite to cause a stir. I don't think they did, but I don't know if that was the case but certainly from my conversation I got the impression from the partner that he was not inclined to take it any further.*

That's where I came back to the firm [who the individual trained with] *because fortunately the second job I had* [after qualifying] *was as group accountant who were a client of* [the accountancy firm] *so I dealt with a partner there who just also happened to be the firm's HR partner at the time. I rang him to ask if he would*

> *be a referee for me in a new job application because it was clear I wouldn't get a reference from my existing employer. At which point he said why don't you come back to the firm.*

He then reflected on this and how it had turned out well in the end:

> *Yes … because clearly it would be difficult to get a decent reference from the group I was working with. … it was a tricky time. You wouldn't say my career … exactly flying at that moment … I remember walking back across …* [location] *that Friday afternoon thinking well I haven't got a job and I've got a mortgage and two kids.*

In the context of such a situation, a retired Big 4 partner stated that:

> *The key element is helping someone who is at the start or the middle of a problem do the right thing, without losing your job and prospects … the key is knowing how and who to feed things into … you need to make sure that you feed things into the Chair of the Audit Committee, or if he is too close to the action, someone on the Board because ultimately these things are board responsibilities, who will understand the issue … but not in writing … you may need to ring ICAS and tell them what you have done and then start looking for another job.*

and he continued:

> *Once you are looking at whistle blowing and strengthening procedures for protecting whistle blowing you are at the last ditch effort/remedy side of things … whistle blowing only happens when everything else has been ineffective.*

Thus, the support proposed in Table 6.4 may be a vital way of avoiding whistle blowing situations. Giving advice on how to avoid confrontations would ensure that the ethically right outcome was achieved and improve the chances that individuals were able to remain in their jobs.

Regulation and governance processes

Society in the past has held the profession in esteem and, as a result, has granted the profession privileges such as a statutory monopoly on audit. From this self-regulation, where market forces influenced professional reputations and the work that accountants did, the profession has moved to a statutory-regulated, rules-based environment, with the introduction of the 8th Directive by the European Union, the establishment of the Financial Reporting Council (FRC) in the UK and the Sarbanes-Oxley Act in the US. Most of this regulation has been intended to serve the public interest, and has responded to significant incidents in recent years that have impaired the reputation of the profession. In comparison with other professions, accountants have a far wider brief and need to consider the client, their firm or business, the profession and the regulatory environment as well as the public interest. Other professions, such as lawyers, only have the interests of their clients to consider.

One way to increase the respect of the accountancy profession is to enhance its ability to follow up the shortcomings identified by other bodies and regulators and Table 6.5 reports the respondents' views on this. For example, the questionnaire respondents believed that if a company had to correct its accounts as a result of intervention by the Financial Reporting Review Panel (FRRP) then both accountants in the company and the accounting firms servicing that company should be subject to scrutiny by their professional body. This step was seen as viable, as noted by a retired Big 4 partner, drawing from his experience with how institutions dealt with ethical and/or legal breaches:

Let me give you an example ... I was involved in a company and there was a rumour of a bid ... just before the bid was announced the share price moved up. Within 48 hours I had a letter from the Stock Exchange Listing authority asking me to fill in a form and to indicate who (if anyone) I had shared this information with. I was quite shocked to realise that the Stock Exchange was following things so closely but impressed too that they were taking insider dealing seriously.

Thus, punishing poor financial reporting may have support within the accountancy profession as a whole.

Table 6.5: Financial reporting governance processes

	Percentage of respondents agreeing or strongly agreeing with these statements
The Institutes should follow up the finance directors of companies that have been criticised by the Financial Reporting Review Panel	80
The Institutes should follow up firms that have been criticised by the Financial Reporting Review Panel	80
The exercise of existing consultation rights by audit committees will improve ethical standards	40

The exercise of consultation rights by audit committees also found some favour with questionnaire respondents. The role of audit committees was also linked to the strengthening of the corporate governance framework. For example, a member in business noted:

I think that corporate governance is an important issue but corporate governance to me suggests a sort of quite a formal type regime which I'm sure is very important and certainly in public companies it has increased in the last few years. There is also to me a duty on the people running the companies to behave in certain ways and adopt certain standards, I suppose. Again you are always going to get the rogues and people who are around to steal and cheat and I suppose you need the regulators; you need the auditors to come in and catch those.

However, another respondent commented that it was difficult to implement procedures that would catch everyone:

There are always going to be the bad people around who are always going to try and circumvent the rules and try and get away with stuff like stealing and things so, it is like, there are always burglars around. The vast majority of people are not burglars. I think it is going to be very difficult to impose such standards … [such as] *you can't become a part of management or a company director unless you pass an ethical test. I can't really see that happening. Then I suppose you're talking about, to make them more accountable, and then you are talking about more control over them, I suppose you are into, then, developing more formal structures in terms of corporate governance to do that.*

Further, a partner in a medium-sized firm argued that no matter how good the regulatory structure and procedures were, at the end of the day it was the professional integrity of the individual that mattered:

I am concerned that the debate leads to a further bolstering of the governance structure rather than relating to individual integrity and the application of personal standards consistently applied within an overall framework of general principles. There is no substitute for personal integrity. My submission is based on many years' experience as Financial Director in public companies and more recently as a partner in a professional practice.

Thus, although the exercise of consultation rights by audit committees may improve ethical standards to some extent, there was not enough support for a recommendation to the Financial Reporting Council to make changes to the Combined Code.

Summary

A number of recommendations have emerged from this chapter and are outlined below:

1. Member support services should be promoted more actively, with publicity designed to ensure that all members are kept aware of its existence.
2. Member support services should feature regularly in professional publications.
3. Help sheets, frequently asked questions with solutions and other supporting information should be posted on websites and be readily available by fax or email.
4. Dedicated ethics teams should be established, possibly across all the professional bodies.
5. Institutes should provide mentors to members who are in particularly difficult situations.
6. Soundings should be taken on whether a service should be provided to give advice to those who are grappling with ethical concerns, and who could refer to this advice in their *CVs* if they lost their jobs.

7. Non-political bodies, such as the Institute of Business Ethics, should be consulted to investigate the extent to which outside expertise could enhance professional accountants' ethics.
8. The Codes of Conduct should be enforced through a more transparent disciplinary process.
9. The professional bodies should develop a detailed summary of disciplinary complaints arising from all the professional accounting bodies.
10. Soundings should be taken to decide whether statutory recognition for Codes of Conduct should be sought.
11. Accountants who are implicated in revisions of company accounts following FRRP investigations should be investigated by their professional body.

This part of the report has examined the remedies that could be introduced to improve the ethical decision making of accountants. At the end of each of the last three chapters a series of recommendations have been made for future consultation. The final chapter attempts to bring together the findings of this report.

Chapter Seven

Conclusions and Recommendations

Introduction

The purpose of this report has been to examine critically and reflect upon the extent to which ethical standards are being upheld by accountants, regardless of whether they work in a professional practice or in business. This examination has been prompted, in part, by the public's perception that accountants' behaviour has been found lacking in recent, high profile, corporate collapses. The report also responds to the need for a professional accounting body, such as ICAS, to periodically review its ethical standards, to ensure that they are being adhered to and that appropriate steps are being taken to support members upholding those standards. This twin purpose has resulted in the report having a strong diagnostic element, in Part One, as well as a number of recommendations, in Part Two.

From the data gathered in interviews and from a questionnaire survey, there appears to be a widespread recognition of the need for sound ethical performance. The majority of those who took part in the study had their own ethical stance which they articulated with varying degrees of formality. Their ways of thinking about ethics and ethical decision-making frameworks were consistent with professional codes of ethics. In addition, a number of individuals applied a principles-based framework to ethical decision making. What was striking, however, was the diversity of the ethical frames of reference that were being used, and the extent to which some of these were possibly idiosyncratic and individualised. The professional environment of accountants appears to have sensitised them to the need to 'take ethics to heart', but each individual has a subtly different view of what that means in practice.

There is evidence that an accountant's work provides considerable scope for ethical challenges. This is unsurprising given the complexity of an accountant's role in business and the importance of financial information in governing small and large-scale business organisations. However, how, where and when 'good' ethical decisions are made is not directly observable. Nevertheless it is possible to draw together a number of insights about how accountants incorporate ethics into their working lives, to provide the context within which the recommendations of this report are framed.

The ethical landscape

In seeking to understand how accountants take ethics to heart, the report has explicitly placed the individual accountant at the core of its conceptualisation of decision making. In this respect, the report assumes that individual accountants, because of their training and socialisation, have the power to make, or not make, the 'right' decisions from an ethical perspective; individual accountants should exercise their responsibility to behave in an ethical fashion. Accountants should have the ability to know what is 'right' from their education and training. Knowledge of a code of conduct, and an appreciation of how key ethical principles translate into ethically sound decisions are, therefore, at the core of maintaining the accounting profession's ethical standards.

The report broadens its perspective from individuals to consider the context within which accountants work. The work environment, the culture and the socialisation processes within it, influence an individual's ethical decision making. Within the work environment there are both formal and informal processes which combine together to form the ethical culture. The informal processes are hard to document and identify in a systematic manner. The formal procedures, however, can be investigated and include: ethical training in the workplace; the use of in-house ethics manuals; mentors; annual ethics sign-offs; escalation processes for ethical dilemmas; and ethics partners and ethics officers. These processes may operate within professional accounting firms or businesses. However, sole accountants within business, or sole practitioners, may at times feel isolated and require special support from their professional accountancy bodies in order to continue to act with the highest level of integrity.

A distinctive finding which emerges from this study is the suggestion that, for many accountants, ethics begins to 'bite' at particular times within a career. In particular, during the early stages of a career relatively few ethical challenges present themselves, and there are usually clear supporting mechanisms for individuals to use to ensure that the 'right' decisions are made, usually by way of referring decisions upwards. Thus, while an awareness of what ethics entails is essential for all accountants, in the early stages of an accounting career the need to exercise ethical judgement is relatively limited.

A change arises at the level of becoming a manager in a firm or at the level just below director in a business organisation. At this stage the complexity of the decisions to be taken, and the potential consequences of those decisions, are much greater. Further, the individual accountant may be encountering these issues and tensions for the first time.

The above observations are drawn together in Table 7.1 which draws an ethics timeline over an accountant's career to highlight the time when it is likely to be critical for additional attention to be paid to ethical performance. It is also at this time when poor ethical decisions may begin to have a potentially serious impact on, for example, the capital markets if the decision affects the quality of financial information.

Table 7.1: The ethical landscape

High

Perceived ethical complexity

Low

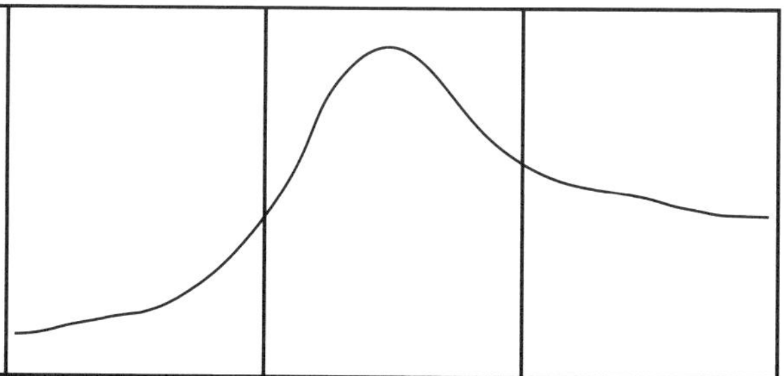

	Stage 1	**Stage 2**	**Stage 3**
General description of phase for an accountant in a professional firm	From trainee accountant stage until manager	From manager to partner	Experienced practitioners in their field
General description of phase for an accountant in business	From trainee accountant to lower/middle management	Middle management up to direct report to a director	Senior management, such as Finance Director
Risk description	Low inherent risk because: (i) decisions are unlikely to have major consequences; and (ii) the individual is likely to work in a well structured environment with good support mechanisms.	High risk as the complexity of the job increases and difficult issues are faced for the first time with, pressure from above to perform and meet targets.	Medium/high risk as the stakes may be high but experience and seniority help to counteract pressure.

	Stage 1	Stage 2	Stage 3
Possible approach to ethical problems	Use a principles-based approach that is intuitive and is largely untested by circumstances.	Adopt a rules-based approach to cope with multiple pressures and complex and ambiguous situations.	Revert to a principles-based approach where judgements are informed by experience, and the maturity and personal confidence to deal with situations.
Education needs	Needs to be sensitised to ethical decision making and made aware that pressure will increase over time.	Guidance for complex real-world situations with large potential positive, and negative, payoffs, using an applied framework for ethical decision making.	Training should focus on refreshing knowledge, including inculcating ethical standards into others.
Organisations' supporting roles	Sensitise employees to ethical issues and the standards expected.	Provide support for individuals as they reach key levels as they are promoted through the organisation.	Refresh and reinforce the need for ethical standards and ensure that mechanisms are in place to support ethical decision making.

Note: The above table is based on the progress of an acountant from trainee through to being a senior member of the profession. While not all trainees will eventually progress to partner/director levels, the basic principle of development through different stages will still apply.

The report examines a number of remedies to ensure that appropriate mechanisms are in place to ensure 'good' decision making. A common theme from the interviews and questionnaires is that the 'tone from the top' of any organisation is crucial to ensuring sound ethical decision making. Having appropriate mechanisms in place to encourage ethical behaviour is a necessary condition, but not a sufficient one, for ethical behaviour. This was eloquently expressed by a retired Big 4 partner who stated:

> *I think it doesn't matter how good your rules are if you are going to have people that are going to skirt around it. If you've got courses and you force someone to go to them if they are unethical, all you are doing is you are making them sit there whilst they listen to somebody tell them how to behave. You are always going to get those who flout the rules or look for ways around it. All we can do is put the tools in place and encouragement and reinforce standards from a very early time and obviously have sanctions against that if they walk away from the company.*

The conceptualisation of the accountant's ethical time-line in Table 7.1 only considers the accountant's work environment. However, the research report also addresses the broader regulatory and institutional framework within which accountants operate and considers the extent to which existing, or new, mechanisms could provide a more supportive environment for the maintenance of ethical standards. Partners in such a process include the Financial Reporting Review Panel which, as part of its remit, identifies organisations where inappropriate financial accounting decisions have been made. In these instances, it is possible that there have been ethical failures which should be investigated by the individual accountant's professional accounting body. To implement this process, changes to the current regulatory environment would need to take place. Similarly, there is little scope for individual institutes to review the extent to which professional accounting firms have appropriate mechanisms in place, for example, processes that ensure that audit partners cannot override technical advice. The appropriate oversight of these processes is likely to require a much less formalised approach than with the FRRP.

A summary of the recommendations

The recommendations in this report have been shaped by an understanding of the ethical landscape within which individual accountants work. Detailed recommendations are contained at the end of chapters four to six and are not re-produced in full here. Instead, the recommendations are re-cast in terms of those who should take action: individual accountants; professional accountancy firms; business organisations; ICAS; all professional accountancy bodies; and regulatory agencies. Table 7.2 summarises the pattern of joint and individual responsibilities of these entities as they relate to the recommendations contained in the report.

Table 7.2 Linking recommendations to actions

	Responsibility for action		
Chapter 4	**The individual accountant**	**Professional accountancy firms**	**Business organisations generally**
Review ethics training within professional accountancy programmes		√	√
Develop realistic, practical education material for ethics education		√	√
Identify and teach an appropriate decision-making framework		√	√
Examine ethics during the qualification process			
Firms and businesses should structure ethical training for all levels of seniority		√	√
Accounting professionals should be sensitised to ethics in the workplace	√	√	√
Training should ensure that individuals recognise ethical issues when they arise		√	√
Deliver ethics and CPD education when ethics begins to "bite"	√	√	√
Ethics should be linked to accountants' career development plans, team working and projects	√	√	√

	Responsibility for action		
Chapter 4	**ICAS**	**ICAS in partnership with other bodies***	**ICAS in partnership with regulatory agencies**
Review ethics training within professional accountancy programmess	√	√	
Develop realistic, practical education material for ethics education	√	√	
Identify and teach an appropriate decision-making framework	√	√	
Examine ethics during the qualification process	√	√	
Firms and businesses should structure ethical training for all levels of seniority	√	√	
Accounting professionals should be sensitised to ethics in the workplace			
Training should ensure that individuals recognise ethical issues when they arise	√	√	
Deliver ethics and CPD education when ethics begins to "bite"	√	√	
Ethics should be linked to accountants' career development plans, team working and projects			

* Other bodies include other professional accountancy bodies, universities and accounting educators

	Responsibility for action		
Chapter 5	**The individual accountant**	**Professional accountancy firms**	**Business organisations generally**
Documenting and evaluating risk management using an ethical performance framework		√	√
Emphasising the 'tone from the top'		√	√
Ethical code of practices should be stated in organisational handbooks		√	√
Recruitment, training and evaluation based on ethics and best practice knowledge		√	√
Appraisal and promotion processes should include self-assessments on ethics		√	√
Introduce prizes or rewards for good ethical decision making		√	√
Establish escalation processes to help resolve ethical dilemmas		√	√
Ethics partners/officers should be established in organisations		√	√
Consider the introduction of incidents books		√	√
Institutes should facilitate a forum to share experiences			
Institutes should facilitate the dissemination of best practice			
Technical staff dominate audit partners over complex issues		√	
Risk management should be separated from business performance		√	

	Responsibility for action		
Chapter 5	**ICAS**	**ICAS in partnership with other bodies**	**ICAS in partnership with regulatory agencies**
Documenting and evaluating risk management using an ethical performance framework	√	√	
Emphasising the 'tone from the top'			
Ethical code of practices should be stated in organisational handbooks			
Recruitment, training and evaluation based on ethics and best practice knowledge			
Appraisal and promotion processes should include self-assessments on ethics			
Introduce prizes or rewards for good ethical decision making	√	√	
Establish escalation processes to help resolve ethical dilemmas			
Ethics partners/officers should be established in organisations	√	√	√
Consider the introduction of incidents books			
Institutes should facilitate a forum to share experiences	√	√	
Institutes should facilitate the dissemination of best practice	√	√	
Technical staff dominate audit partners over complex issues			
Risk management should be separated from business performance			

	Responsibility for action		
Chapter 5	**The individual accountant**	**Professional accountancy firms**	**Business organisations generally**
Audit committees should review ethical practices			√
Internal audit should review ethical issues			√
Professional codes of conduct should reflect the work of members in business as well as in practice			

	Responsibility for action		
Chapter 5	**ICAS**	**ICAS in partnership with other bodies**	**ICAS in partnership with regulatory agencies**
Audit committees should review ethical practices			
Internal audit should review ethical issues			
Professional codes of conduct should reflect the work of members in business as well as in practice	√	√	

	Responsibility for action		
Chapter 6	**The individual accountant**	**Professional accountancy firms**	**Business organisations generally**
Promote member services			
Feature member services in professional publications			
Provide help sheets and other information			
Establish dedicated ethics teams			
Provide mentors to members in difficult ethical situations	√		
Establish an ethical advice service which could be referred to in CVs			
Non-political bodies should be consulted on ethics			
Enforce Codes of Conduct through a more transparent disciplinary process			
Summarise disciplinary procedures and penalties across institutes			
Investigate statutory recognition for codes of conduct			
Investigate conduct of accountants implicated in revisions of company accounts following FRRP investigations.			

	Responsibility for action		
Chapter 6	**ICAS**	**ICAS in partnership with other bodies**	**ICAS in partnership with regulatory agencies**
Promote member services	√	√	
Feature member services in professional publications	√	√	
Provide help sheets and other information	√	√	
Establish dedicated ethics teams	√	√	
Provide mentors to members in difficult ethical situations	√	√	
Establish an ethical advice service which could be referred to in CVs	√	√	
Non-political bodies should be consulted on ethics	√	√	
Enforce Codes of Conduct through a more transparent disciplinary process	√	√	
Summarise disciplinary procedures and penalties across institutes	√	√	
Investigate statutory recognition for codes of conduct	√	√	√
Investigate conduct of accountants implicated in revisions of company accounts following FRRP investigations.	√	√	√

Taken together, the recommendations do not propose radically new modes of operation but seek to create an environment where individual accountants, the organisations which employ them and the professional accountancy bodies of which they are members seek to re-sensitise themselves to the ethical standards demanded.

There are specific sets of recommendations which require action in the future and these focus on:

- The education and training of ethics. ICAS, IFAC and other accounting bodies are already working in this area and this report seeks to influence their pronouncements.
- Mechanisms for supporting ethical practices within organisations. A more widespread understanding of these processes, how an effective 'tone from the top' can be implemented, and how to enshrine ethical principles within organisations all feature within this report's recommendations.
- New institutional arrangements. New regulatory and institutional practices should be investigated to reinforce the ethical standards of accountants.

These three sets of recommendations are complementary in nature. Taking ethics to heart is not a simple task, nor is it an impossible task. Individual accountants and the profession have the depth and breadth of experience to achieve ethical decision making. There is, however, a need to remain proactive in seeking to ensure that the accounting profession upholds the standards for which it has been granted professional status.

References

Armstrong, M B (1987), "Moral development and accounting education", *Journal of Accounting Education*, Spring, pp.27-44.

Auditing Practices Board (2003), *Draft Ethical Standards for Auditors*, Auditing Practices Board, London.

Bromell, T (2004), "Taking an Ethical Lead", *Accountancy Magazine*, Sept, pp.131-141.

Chaiken, S and C Stangor (1987), "Attitude and Attitude Change", *Annual Review of Psychology*, Vol.38, pp.575-630.

Department of Trade and Industry (2004), *Draft Regulations on the Operating and Financial Review and Directors' Report A consultative document,* Department of Trade and Industry, London.

Donaldson, J (1988), *Key Issues in Business Ethics,* Academic Press: London.

Dunn, J, J McKernan and P O'Donnell (2003), *Moral Reasoning and the Accountant: Rules and Principles,* Certified Accountants Educational Trust, London.

Gray, R, J Bebbington and K McPhail (1994), "Teaching Ethics in Accounting and the Ethics of Accounting Teaching: Education for Immorality and the Case for Social and Environmental Accounting Education", *Accounting Education* 3(1), pp.51-75.

Institute of Chartered Accountants of Scotland (1997), *Guide to Professional Ethics,* Institute of Chartered Accountants of Scotland, Edinburgh.

Institute of Chartered Accountants of Scotland (2003), *Fast Forward to 2010,* Institute of Chartered Accountants of Scotland, Edinburgh.

International Federation of Accountants (2003), *IES 1 Entry Requirements to a Program of Professional Accounting Education,* International Federation of Accountants, New York.

International Federation of Accountants (2003), *IES 2 Content of Professional Accounting Education Programs,* International Federation of Accountants, New York.

International Federation of Accountants (2003), *IES 3 Professional Skills,* International Federation of Accountants, New York.

International Federation of Accountants (2003), *IES 4 Professional Values Ethics and Attitudes,* International Federation of Accountants, New York.

International Federation of Accountants (2003), *IES 5 Practical Experience Requirements,* International Federation of Accountants, New York.

International Federation of Accountants (2003), *IES 6 Assessment of Professional Capabilities and Competence,* International Federation of Accountants, New York.

International Federation of Accountants (2004), *IES 7 Continuing Professional Development:A Program of Lifelong Learning and Continuing Development of Professional Competence,* International Federation of Accountants, New York.

International Federation of Accountants (2003), *Proposed Revised Code of Ethics for Professional Accountants,* International Federation of Accountants, New York.

Lovell, A (forthcoming), *Ethics in Business*, Institute of Chartered Accountants of Scotland, Edinburgh.

McPhail, K (forthcoming), *Ethics and the Individual Professional,* Institute of Chartered Accountants of Scotland, Edinburgh.

Mozier, P (1991), "Independence" in M Sherer and S Turley (Eds), *Current Issues in Auditing,* 2nd ed, Paul Chapman, London.

New Oxford Shorter English Dictionary (1993).

Pierce, A (forthcoming), *Ethics and the Professional Accounting Firm,* Institute of Chartered Accountants of Scotland, Edinburgh.

Ponemon, L A (1990), "Ethical judgment in accounting: a cognitive-developmental perspective", *Critical Perspectives on Accounting,* pp.191-215.

Ponemon, L A (1992a), "Ethical reasoning and selection-socialization in accounting", *Accounting, Organisations and Society*, pp.239-58.

Ponemon, L A (1992b), "Auditor under-reporting of time and moral reasoning, an experimental lab study", *Contemporary Accounting Research*, pp.171-89.

Rest, J (1979), *Development in Judging Moral Issues*, University of Minnesota Press, Minneapolis.

Rest, J (1986), *DIT: Manual for the Defining Issues Test*, University of Minnesota Press, Minneapolis.

Tricker, B (2002), "Auditing: profession or business?", *Accountancy*, p.79.

Walker, S P (1991), "The Defence of Professional Monopoly: Scottish Chartered Accountants and 'Satellites in the Accounting Firmament' 1854-1914", *Accounting, Organisations and Society*, 16(3), pp.257-283.

Zeff, S A (2003), "How the U.S. Accounting Profession Got Where It Is Today: Part II", *Accounting Horizons*.

Appendix One

Research Methods and Research Instruments

In this appendix the research instruments used in the report are reproduced. Two main data gathering processes were used; interviews and a questionnaire survey. Descriptions of who were interviewed and questionnaire respondents' profiles can be found in Chapter One of the report.

Table A1.1 reproduces the questions asked during interviews with accountants. The questions that were asked differed according to the environment in which the interviewee worked; in professional practice or in business, and this distinction has been highlighted in the table. In addition, Table A1.2 reproduces the questions asked of other professional bodies.

The following pages reproduce the questionnaire materials: including the letter to ICAS members and the questionnaire itself.

Table A1.1: Interview questions (for accountant in professional practice and in business)

General background

1. What is your definition of ethics?
2. Is there a difference between professional ethics and ethics in general, and if so, can you give me an example?
3. Do different cultural backgrounds, culture, organisational settings affect views on ethics?
4. Do ethical views change over time? For example:
5. Would a child have the same ethical stance as an adult?
6. Would a junior manager have the same ethical stance as a senior executive?

Professional ethics

7. What are professional ethics?
8. What are the differences between integrity, objectivity, professional competence, due care, confidentiality and professional behaviour?
9. Is independence a key feature of professional ethics?
10. Do you agree with the APB's definition of threats to ethics being self-interest; advocacy; management; self-review; familiarity; and intimidation?
11. Apart from Enron, can you give me any examples of ethical breakdowns and why ethical codes were breached?
12. What ethical values can be learnt from the Enron saga?
13. Are there any organisations or types of business that you consider to be ethical and why?
14. Are there any organisations or types of business that you consider to be unethical and why?
15. Is there a difference in maintaining an ethical stance depending upon whether an accountant is in business or in practice?

Accountants in practice

16. Does the culture of the firm affect the ethical stance of individuals within the firm?
17. Does joint and several liability have a bearing on ethics within practice?
18. Is there a difference between small and large practices?
19. Are multi-disciplinary practices a threat to professional ethics?
20. What about non-audit services? Should any be allowed, and if so, in what circumstances?
21. Do you agree think that the APB's advice to have an ethics partner and independent partners in practice will improve professional ethics?
22. Should audit partners be rotated, and if so, after how long - 5 years as proposed by the APB?
23. How does confidentiality affect members in practice?
24. How should practices treat "dubious" clients - is it better to give them at least some service rather than having an underclass of businesses with no professional services?
25. If a client was known to be doing something "illegal" or not best practice, what steps should the accountant take?
26. How do accountants in practice resolve any ethical problems?
27. Have you come across any ethical issues yourself - either your own or of colleagues/friends?
28. Do firms have their own ethics manuals and/or ethical advice services?

Accountants in Business

29. What sort of problems arise for members in business?
30. Have you come across any ethical issues yourself - either your own or of colleagues/friends?
31. Is the accountant embedded in their organisation and adopts the culture of that organisation?

32. Are there different issues depending upon whether it is a large or small organisation and whether any other accountants or professionals work there also?
33. If an accountant knew that something did not appear to be "right" what steps should that accountant take?
34. How do accountants in practice resolve any ethical problems?
35. Do firms have their own ethics manuals and/or ethical advice services?

Remedies

36. Should firms or professional bodies have a mechanism whereby members can raise concerns or whistle-blow?
37. Should there be an independent service established for concerns to be aired?
38. Should firms/professional bodies have ethical guides that the courts could follow?
39. Should firms/bodies promote aspirational behaviour, and if so, how?
40. Should the self-interest of individuals be aligned to ethics, and if so how?
41. To what extent should ethics be part of education and training and what form should this take - case studies/prior cases/focus on greed/power etc?
42. Can recruitment and selection and promotion of staff be aligned with ethics, and if so how?
43. Can anything be learnt from other professions or professional bodies?
44. Is there any way that ethics guidelines could be validated?

Table A1.2: Interview questions (for representatives of other institutes)

Ethics in general

1. Could you please explain your role at the Institute?
2. What is your definition of ethics?
3. Is there a difference between professional ethics and ethics in general, and if so, can you give me an example?
4. Do different cultural backgrounds, culture, organisational settings affect views on ethics?
5. Do ethical views change over time? For example:
6. Would a child have the same ethical stance as an adult?
7. Would a junior manager have the same ethical stance as a senior executive?
8. Are there any organisations or types of business that you consider to be ethical and why?
9. Are there any organisations or types of business that you consider to be unethical and why?

Professional bodies

10. What processes exist to establish an ethical framework for Institute members to operate within?
11. Should firms/professional bodies have ethical guides that the courts could follow?
12. Is there any way that ethics guidelines could be validated?
13. To what extent should ethics be part of education, training and CPD and what form should this take - case studies/prior cases/ focus on greed/power etc?
14. How are members updated for changes to ethics standards?
15. Should professional bodies promote aspirational behaviour, and if so, how?

16. Should the self-interest of individuals be aligned to ethics, and if so how?
17. Can admission to the Institute be aligned with ethics, and if so how?
18. In an ideal world what would the Institute do with respect to creating and maintaining the ethical standards of its members?
19. Can anything be learnt from other professions or professional bodies?

Member services

20. Should firms or professional bodies have a mechanism whereby members can raise concerns or whistle-blow?
21. Should there be an independent service established for concerns to be aired?
22. What member services are offered with respect to ethical guidance - phone, e-mail, fax?
23. What prompts people to contact the Institute?
24. What sort of problems do they ask about?
25. What sort of remedies do you suggest to maintain professional ethics?
26. Are there help sheets for members about ethical dilemmas?
27. Is there a central recording system of the calls and problems and what sort of records are kept?

Disciplinary hearings

28. What triggers a disciplinary hearing for the Institute?
29. What are the typical ethical problems that present themselves to the Institute that result in disciplinary hearings?
30. What are the typical actions that result?
31. What publicity is undertaken for Institute members who have broken ethical standards?
32. Is it important to publicise breaches of ethical standards?

33. What triggers a change or re-consideration of ethical issues at the Institute?
34. Did Enron, or any of the other scandals, trigger the Institute to reflect on its practices with respect to ethics?

The following pages reproduce the questionnaire materials: including the letter to ICAS members and the questionnaire itself.

CVH/IW

«Name»
«JobTitle»
«CompanyName»
«StreetAddress»
«PostTown»
«PostCode»

7 April 2004

Dear «Salutation»

TAKING ETHICS TO HEART

The Research Committee of the Institute of Chartered Accountants of Scotland is currently devoting significant resources to a project that is examining the ethical standing of accountants. The project has been prompted, in part, by recent controversies that have diminished the standing of accountants in the eyes of the general public. Whilst recognising that in the vast majority of cases appropriate standards are being maintained, the study is examining, *inter alia*, ways in which the business and commercial environment places accountants, wherever they work, under pressure to make decisions and judgements that may lead to poor ethical standards being maintained.

In brief, the research being undertaken is seeking to:

- document the pressures that accountants face in ensuring ethical standards are maintained; and
- explore the ways in which ICAS may respond creatively to the pressures its members are under.

The findings of the work will be of relevance to ICAS and to the accountancy profession in general. The findings from this project will be published to coincide with the 150th anniversary of the Institute in the autumn. The robustness and validity of this research relies upon ICAS members taking an active part in contributing their views to the research. To this end we would greatly appreciate your support in the project by responding to the questionnaire which is attached to this letter. A freepost envelope is enclosed and the questionnaire should take approximately 20 minutes to complete. We should be grateful if you would return the completed questionnaire to us by **Monday 26 April, 2004**.

Thank you for your support.

With very best wishes,

Yours sincerely

Professor Christine Helliar
Director of Research

THE
INSTITUTE OF
CHARTERED
ACCOUNTANTS
OF SCOTLAND

Taking Ethics to Heart

INTRODUCTION TO THE QUESTIONNAIRE

This questionnaire is designed to elicit views from ICAS members about the ethical standing of accountants working in public practice and in business. The questionnaire will feed into related research work that is being undertaken in conjunction with the 150th anniversary of the formation of ICAS.

The questionnaire is aimed at accountants in public practice and working in business and includes questions on the nature of the ethical issues that present themselves to accountants, and also considers how ICAS can continue to support its members and ensure that they are able to, and continue to, aspire to the highest ethical standards.

In order to refresh your memory, a brief summary of the Institute's Professional Code of Conduct for members is attached at the end of this questionnaire.

Please place ticks in the boxes that correspond most closely to your PERSONAL views, as they are developed and informed by the work that you do as an accountant.

SECTION A – BACKGROUND INFORMATION

The information in this section will be used for analytical purposes only.

If your career has been mainly or wholly in professional practice please complete questions one, two and three. If you work in business please complete questions four, five and six.

1. **Please indicate your position in the organisation**

Partner ☐ Manager ☐ Qualified-other ☐ Retired ☐ (Please complete questions two and three in respect of your main employment during your working life, then go to section B)

2. **Firm size**

Sole practitioner ☐ 2-20 partners ☐ 21+ partners (non Big 4) ☐

Big 4 ☐

3. **How many years have you worked for your organisation?**

Less than 1 ☐ 1-5 ☐ 6-10 ☐ 11-15 ☐ More than 15 ☐

Please go to section B.

4. **Please state your position in the organisation**

Director ☐ Manager ☐ Other ☐ Retired ☐ (Please complete questions five and six in respect of your main employment during your working life, then go to section B)

5. **Company size by turnover**

Less than £100m ☐ £100m-£500m ☐ £501m-£1bn ☐

More than £1bn ☐

Company sector
Please state your organisation's main area of business (*eg* electronics, food, manufacturing, telecommunications)

____

6. How many years have you worked for your organisation?

Less than 1	1-5	6-10	11-15	More than 15
☐	☐	☐	☐	☐

SECTION B – PROFESSIONAL ACCOUNTANTS

7. The following problems have been suggested as creating situations that may lead to ethical dilemmas for professional accountants, with the potential for poor ethical decision making, which ultimately could lead to an individual professional accountant behaving unethically. We would stress, however, that we are not assuming that an ethical dilemma will necessarily lead to a poor decision being made, or that a reduction in ethical standards will occur. Indeed, we recognise that in the majority of difficult situations individual accountants make sound decisions with sound ethical outcomes. What we wish to uncover is the extent to which you agree that the following situations can lead to pressures that may result in unethical behaviour, based on your **own experience** of such conflicts/pressures/problems in your own working life.

Problem/Pressure/Situation
Lack of personal confidence in being able to say "no"
Peer pressure to conform to current practice
Loyalty to a boss or to colleagues
Pressure from superiors
Pressure from clients or customers
Close relationships with clients/customers
Conflict of duties or interests
A lack of a positive leadership or role model
Situations where the benefits on offer appear to be greater than the expected consequences of detection
A commercial culture in a firm or business where results are more important than how they are achieved
Personal greed or self interest may create unethical behaviour
A lack of financial independence hinders an independent view being taken
Pressure to behave unethically is greatest in smaller organisations
Pressure to behave unethically is greatest in larger organisations

1 = strongly agree with statement and 5 = strongly disagree with statement. If you have no experience of the situation described please tick the final column.					
1	2	3	4	5	I have no experience of this

8. There are a number of suggestions as to how a professional accountancy body, such as ICAS, and its members acting as professionals, could counteract the problems listed in the previous table. Please indicate to what extent you believe that these suggestions would reduce the probability of the problems identified in question 7 leading to ethical breaches.

Reminder: the Professional Code of Conduct is reproduced at the end of this questionnaire.

Suggestions for reducing the probability that pressures will lead to unethical behaviour
The profession should establish peer discussion groups
The profession should provide a discussion forum through the Institute of Business Ethics, or a similar body
The existing informal and voluntary ICAS counselling service should advertise its services more effectively
The profession should seek to provide members with a mentor if requested
ICAS and other institutes should provide an in-house service to potential whistle-blowers* even if membership fees had to increase to fund this service
Members consulting this service and subsequently losing their jobs should be able to state on their CVs that they had consulted ICAS and that a record of the matter(s) and the relevant date(s) was documented
ICAS, and other institutes, should provide an independent external service to potential whistle-blowers even if membership fees had to increase to fund this service
ICAS, and other institutes, should offer an insurance service to members for losing a job through whistle-blowing even if membership fees had to increase to fund this service
All members of the profession should sign a "Hippocratic" type oath linked to the Professional Code of Conduct upon being admitted to membership for the first time
All members of ICAS and other institutes should sign an annual certificate confirming that they had complied with the ethics code (see summary at end of this questionnaire)
Compulsory Continuing Professional Development (CPD) training on ethics should be introduced
Members should be required to take self assessment CPD tests on-line
Role play, cameos and case studies on ethics should be part of education and CPD
The education and training about ethics should be increased by the profession
Ethics should be examined in professional exams – probably by the use of hypothetical scenarios

* This refers to an in-house service to support whistle-blowers.

1 = strongly agree with statement and 5 = strongly disagree with statement.				
1	2	3	4	5

Section C – Professional Audit Firms

9. It has been argued that the change in audit firms from professional partnerships towards businesses has created greater pressure for audit firms which may result in unethical behaviour. The following circumstances have been suggested as increasing the propensity for decisions to be made which compromise professional ethics. If you are working in, or have worked in, a professional audit firm please indicate to what extent you agree that the following circumstances create pressures that may lead to unethical behaviour. Once again, we are not suggesting that there are high levels of such behaviour. Rather we want to gather views on whether or not practical experience indicates that there are circumstances which place pressure on individuals working in accountancy firms.

If you do not consider that you have recent experience of a professional accountancy firm please go directly to Section D.

Circumstances which may increase propensity for unethical behaviour
Accounting standards have increased complexity which has increased the opportunity for unethical behaviour
Interpreting standards for clients increases unethical behaviour
Auditors focus too much on chasing sales resulting in unethical behaviour
The increasing focus in firms on the need for commercial success to enable the income aspirations of partners and staff to be met has led to more unethical behaviour
The increase in non-accountants in firms has adversely altered the ethical environment within firms
The provision of non-audit services has increased unethical behaviour

Please state any particular non-audit services that, in your experience, create frequent or significant dilemmas (*eg* Tax, IT, HR, Management consultancy, corporate finance, *etc*)

____

____

____

1 = strongly agree with statement and 5 = strongly disagree with statement. If you have no experience of the situation described please tick the final column.					
1	2	3	4	5	I have no experience of this

10. There are a number of suggestions as to how professional accountancy firms may create structures and incentives in order to counteract the problems listed in the previous table. Please indicate to what extent you believe that these suggestions would reduce the probability of the problems identified in question 9 leading to ethical breaches.

Suggestions for reducing the probability that circumstances will lead to unethical behaviour
Client acceptance procedures should be reviewed externally from firms
The profession's ethical code of practice should be part of a firm's training
Firms' recruitment processes should seek to assess ethical dimensions
Ethics should be part of a firm's training
All firms should introduce an escalation* process to help professionals resolve ethical dilemmas
Firms should include an assessment of ethical behaviour in their criteria for promotion
Each firm should have a reporting register or "incidents book"
A firm's code of conduct should be externally monitored
Audit partners should not be able to make complex technical decisions without reference to specialist technical staff within the firm, or externally, if necessary.
If a conflict exists between the engagement and the technical partner, the technical partner (or, where appropriate, a partner independent of the engagement) should have dominance
Overall risk management responsibilities should be separated from business performance responsibility within the reporting structures of a firm

* An escalation process refers to an arrangement within a firm through which ethical issues encountered by audit teams or individuals can be raised, discussed and resolved.

1 = strongly agree with statement and 5 = strongly disagree with statement				
1	2	3	4	5

Section D – The Accountant in Business

If you have always worked as an accountant within a professional firm, then please go direct to section E.

11. It is recognised that accountants in business face different circumstances that may result in unethical conduct or unethical decisions being made. These pressures are often business specific and as a result we have not listed all possible pressures/circumstances. Taking into consideration the sense that there may be pressures, please indicate to what extent you believe that suggestions in the table below would increase the probability of accountants working in business maintaining appropriate professional standards.

Suggestions for reducing the probability that pressures/ cirumstances will lead to unethical behaviour
All companies should have an ethical code of practice, clearly stated in their handbooks
All companies should introduce an escalation process* to help professionals resolve ethical dilemmas
All companies should include assessment of ethical behaviour within criteria for promotion
The remuneration policies of companies should promote ethical behaviour
A company's code of conduct should be externally monitored
Audit committees should review ethical practices
Where internal audit exists, its review should extend to ethical issues
Each company should have a reporting register or "incidents book" maintained by a named person
The named person should be responsible for the escalation of matters recorded in the process and incidents book where appropriate: (a) This individual should be a board member (Please state preference below, *eg* HR director/company secretary *etc*) ____________________________________ (b) If the finance director is also the company secretary, should an independent director be the repository
All employers should require all employees to sign an annual ethics certificate
Ethics officers should be appointed in all organisations
Ethics officers should provide a system of formal confirmations to their Boards that state that policy and practice have been monitored and complied with and any variation or non-compliances reported to the Board or a designated Board Committee
Ethical compliance should be reviewed and reported on by the Institute for Business Ethics or an independent body

* An escalation process refers to an arrangement within a company through which ethical issues encountered by individuals can be raised, discussed and resolved.

1 = strongly agree with statements and 5 = strongly disagree with statement.				
1	2	3	4	5

SECTION E – ICAS, OTHER PROFESSIONAL BODIES AND REGULATION

12. It is widely accepted that in the continued drive to ensure that accountants uphold the highest ethical standards, professional bodies have a role to play. The following statements relate to actions and circumstances that are concerned with the broad area of professional body regulation. Please indicate to what extent you agree with the following statements.

The following statements, actions and circumstances relate to the extent to which regulating accounting could affect the ethical performance of the profession
The principles of the profession's Code of Conducts should be given statutory* recognition
The code of conduct should be reviewed regularly
The exercise of existing consultation rights by audit committees improves ethical standards
LLP status improves ethical behaviour
The mandatory rotation of audit partners enhances ethical behaviour
Banning non-audit services by firms would improve ethical standards
Multi-disciplinary practices create additional ethical problems for accountants
The audit profession should be nationalised to improve ethical outcomes in the expectation that this would lead to higher calibre auditors and fewer audit failures
The Institutes should follow up firms whose clients' accounts have been criticised by the Financial Reporting Review Panel
The Institutes should follow up the finance directors of companies whose accounts have been criticised by the Financial Reporting Review Panel

* Statutory recognition refers to professional standards having a standing in law (that is, being legally sanctioned and hence legally enforceable). For example, lawyers' ethical codes have statutory recognition. The suggestion for this arises from the difficulties that exist in enforcing the members' Code of Ethics in the face of challenges from, for example, the Human Rights Act.

1 = strongly agree with statement and 5 = strongly disagree with statement				
1	2	3	4	5

SECTION F

13. Please state your definition of ethics:

14. Do you have a clear decision-making framework that you use to resolve ethical issues, and if so, what are the key elements?

15. If you would like to comment further on this topic, please do so below:

The Institute of Chartered Accountants of Scotland Professional Code of Conduct for Members

The primary duty of The Institute of Chartered Accountants of Scotland is to the public. This principle determines its status as a professional body, distinguishing it from the trade association whose sole concern is the interests of its members. A primary function of the Institute, therefore, is to ensure that the confidence in which the public holds the CA qualification continues to be justified.

It is each member's duty and responsibility to observe high standards of professional conduct at all times. The gravity of this responsibility, particularly in recent years is widely acknowledged, and the Institute has therefore produced a comprehensive Guide for members to assist them in fulfilling their responsibilities as a CA.

Fundamental Principles

1. You should behave with integrity in all professional and business relationships. Integrity implies not merely honesty but fair dealing and truthfulness.
2. You should strive for objectivity in all professional and business judgements. Objectivity is the state of mind which has regard to all considerations relevant to the task in hand but no other.
3. You should not accept or perform work which you are not competent to undertake unless you obtain such advice and assistance as will enable you competently to carry out the work.
4. You should carry out your professional work with due skill, care, diligence and expedition and with proper regard for the technical and professional standards expected of you as a member.

5. You should conduct yourself with courtesy and consideration towards all with whom you come into contact during the course of performing your work.

THANK YOU for your assistance in completing this questionnaire. We should be grateful if you would please return it in the freepost envelope provided, by Monday 26 April 2004.

Appendix Two

A Summary of Responses to the Questionnaire Survey

The following tables restate the questions that were included in the questionnaire survey, together with a statistical analysis of the responses.

Each Table has five columns which show:

- The question.
- No - how many respondents replied to that question.
- Mean - if less than three the respondents agree with the question, if greater than three they disagree.
- Std Dev - the standard deviation shows the diversity in the spread of opinion between the respondents. The higher the value the more diversity there was in the responses.
- P-value - to test whether the response is significantly different from three such that the respondents overall agree or disagree when taking into account the mean value and the standard deviation. A value of less than .05 means that the responses are different from a neutral response of three.

Question 7				
Problem	**No.**	**Mean**	**Std Dev**	**P-value**
Lack of personal confidence in being able to say "no"	136	3.07	1.303	.512
Peer pressure to conform to current practice	134	3.07	1.091	.477
Loyalty to a boss or to colleagues	138	2.98	1.036	.806
Pressure from superiors	135	2.76	1.022	.22
Pressure from clients or customers	129	2.77	1.189	.028
Close relationships with clients/ customers	129	2.99	1.196	.941
Conflict of duties or interests	127	3.14	1.226	.195
A lack of a positive leadership or role model	129	3.16	1.328	.166
Situations where the benefits on offer appear to be greater than the expected consequences of detection	106	3.48	1.304	.000
A commercial culture in the firm where results are more important than how they are achieved	126	2.81	1.361	.119
Personal greed or self interest may create unethical behaviour	116	2.89	1.491	.420
A lack of financial independence hinders an independent view being taken	121	2.93	1.246	.513
Pressure to behave unethically is greatest in smaller organisations	120	4.02	1.195	.000
Pressure to behave unethically is greatest in larger organisations	123	3.48	1.433	.000

Question 8				
Remedy	**No.**	**Mean**	**Std Dev**	**P-value**
The profession should establish peer discussion groups	148	3.13	1.032	.132
The profession should provide a discussion forum through the Institute of Business Ethics, or similar body	149	3.07	0.945	.342
The existing informal and voluntary ICAS counselling service should advertise its services more effectively	148	2.34	1.061	.000
The profession should seek to provide members with a mentor if requested	149	2.53	1.106	.000
ICAS should provide an in-house service to potential whistle-blowers even if membership fees had to increase to fund this service	149	2.79	1.239	.036
Members consulting this service and subsequently losing their jobs could state on their CVs that they had consulted and that ICAS retained a record of the matter(s) covered and the relevant date(s).	148	2.22	1.221	.000
ICAS should provide an independent external service to potential whistle-blowers even if membership fees increased to fund this service	149	2.95	1.164	.613
ICAS should offer an insurance service to members for losing a job through whistle-blowing even if membership fees increased	149	3.17	1.176	.084
All members of the profession should sign a "Hippocratic" type oath linked to the Professional Code of Conduct upon being admitted to membership for the first time	149	2.74	1.269	.015
All ICAS members should sign an annual certificate confirming that they have complied with the ethics code	149	2.79	1.291	.051

Question 8				
Remedy	**No.**	**Mean**	**Std Dev**	**P-value**
Compulsory Continuing Professional Development (CPD) training on ethics should be introduced	148	3.11	1.120	.242
Members should be required to take self assessment CPD tests on-line	148	3.55	1.071	.000
Role play, cameos and case studies on ethics should be part of education and CPD	149	3.16	1.192	.101
The education and training about ethics should be increased by the profession	149	2.56	1.036	.000
Ethics should be examined in professional exams – probably by the use of hypothetical scenarios	148	2.49	1.128	.000

Question 9				
Circumstance	**No.**	**Mean**	**Std Dev**	**P-value**
Accounting standards have increased complexity which has increased the opportunity for unethical behaviour	85	3.19	1.286	.181
Interpreting standards for clients increases unethical behaviour	85	3.36	1.111	.003
Auditors focus too much on chasing sales resulting in unethical behaviour	82	3.24	1.366	.110
The increasing focus in firms on the need for commercial success to enable the income aspirations of partners and staff to be met has led to more unethical behaviour	88	2.95	1.372	.757
The increase in non-accountants in firms has altered the ethical environment within firms adversely	78	3.36	1.269	.015
The provision of non-audit services has increased unethical behaviour.	88	3.09	1.411	.547

Question 10				
Remedy	**No.**	**Mean**	**Std Dev**	**P-value**
Firm's client acceptance procedures should be externally reviewed	101	3.27	1.157	.022
The profession's ethical code of practice should be part of a firm's training	100	1.99	0.798	.000
Firms' recruitment processes should seek to assess ethical dimensions	101	2.51	1.045	.000
Ethics should be part of a firm's training	101	1.94	0.870	.000
All firms should introduce an escalation process to help resolve ethical dilemmas (a process to report up the line)	101	1.89	0.835	.000
Firms should include assessment of ethical behaviour within criteria for promotion	101	2.34	1.032	.000
Each firm should have a reporting register or "incidents book"	101	2.70	1.091	.007
A firm's code of conduct should be externally monitored	101	2.96	1.104	.719
Audit partners should not be able to make complex technical decisions without reference to technical staff	101	2.22	1.064	.000
If a conflict exists within the firm, the technical partner or non-engagement partner should have dominance	100	2.31	0.940	.000
Overall risk management responsibilities should be separated from business performance responsibility within the reporting structures of a firm	101	2.32	0.916	.000

Question 11				
Remedy	**No.**	**Mean**	**Std Dev**	**P-value**
All companies should have an ethical code of practice, clearly stated in their handbooks	84	2.33	1.165	.000
All companies should introduce an escalation process to help professionals resolve ethical dilemmas	84	2.50	1.135	.000
All companies should include assessment of ethical behaviour within criteria for promotion	84	2.68	1.088	.008
The remuneration policies of companies should promote ethical behaviour	83	2.69	1.092	.011
A company's code of conduct should be externally monitored	83	3.16	1.121	.206
Audit committees should review ethical practices	84	2.13	1.159	.000
Where internal audit exists, its review should extend to ethical issues	84	2.23	1.057	.000
Each company should have a reporting register or "incidents book" maintained by a named person	84	2.87	1.210	.324
The named person should be responsible for the escalation process and incidents book.This should be a board member (HR director/company secretary *etc*)	72	2.57	1.276	.006
If the finance director is also the company secretary, an independent director should be the repository	76	2.47	1.311	.001
All employers should require all employees to sign an annual ethics certificate	83	3.46	1.262	.001
Ethics officers should be appointed in all organisations	84	3.61	1.098	.000
Ethics officers should provide a system of formal confirmations to their Boards	84	3.37	1.200	.006
Ethical compliance should be reviewed by the Institute for Business Ethics or an independent body	84	3.49	1.058	.000

Question 12				
Circumstance	**No.**	**Mean**	**Std Dev**	**P-value**
The principles of the profession's Code of Conduct should be given statutory recognition (NB Human Rights)	151	2.66	1.166	.000
The code of conduct should be reviewed regularly	151	1.90	0.746	.000
The exercise of existing consultation rights by audit committees will improve ethical standards	149	2.66	0.920	.000
LLP status improves ethical behaviour	147	3.55	0.938	.000
The mandatory rotation of audit partners enhances ethical behaviour	149	2.70	1.143	.002
Banning non-audit services by firms would improve ethical standards	149	3.15	1.389	.177
Multi-disciplinary practices create additional ethical problems for accountants	150	2.73	1.219	.008
The audit profession should be nationalised to improve ethical outcomes	150	4.25	1.055	.000
The Institutes should follow up firms whose clients' accounts have been criticised by the Financial Reporting Review Panel (FRRP)	151	1.96	0.855	.000
The Institutes should follow up the finance directors of companies that have been criticised by the FRRP	151	1.95	0.915	.000